HIGH
WEALD
WALK

The High Weald Walk has been developed,
interpreted and promoted with the collaboration of the
following Countryside Management Projects:

Kent High Weald Project

The Kent High Weald Project (KHWP) started in 1991, and is a partnership between Kent County Council, Tunbridge Wells Borough Council and the Countryside Commission. The Project focuses on the part of the High Weald Area of Outstanding Natural Beauty (AONB) within Tunbridge Wells Borough, with the aim of enhancing the landscape, conserving natural habitats and improving the amenity value of these areas.

The KHWP also aims to develop opportunities for countryside access and informal recreation, to benefit residents and visitors alike. By encouraging the participation of community groups in project work, local people can be practically involved in caring for and conserving their countryside.

For further information please contact: Kent High Weald Project, Council Offices, High Street, Cranbrook, Kent TN17 3EN, telephone Cranbrook (0580) 712771.

High Weald Conservation Project (East Sussex)

The High Weald Conservation Project (HWCP) is focusing its work and resources in the parishes of Frant, Rotherfield, Wadhurst, Mayfield and Ticehurst in the High Weald AONB in East Sussex. The principal objective of the Project is to conserve and enhance the AONB. To achieve this, the work of the Project includes supporting community participation in maintaining the landscape, wildlife, and resources.
Additionally, the HWCP aims to help maintain the rural economy by providing resources for low key sustainable tourism, such as footpath routes and cycleways.

For further information please contact: The High Weald Conservation Project, Recreation and Countryside Management Service, Southover House, Southover Road, Lewes, East Sussex BN7 1YA, telephone Lewes (0273) 481637.

Along and Around the

HIGH WEALD WALK

Cottages on Southborough Common - Late Summer

Designed and produced by The Design Studio
and Countryside Group, Kent County Council.

Narrative text by Bea Cowan
Landscape illustrations by John Cann
Wildlife studies by Sandra Fernandez
Photographs by Geoffrey King

Maps produced by The Design Studio
with the sanction of the
Controller of HM Stationery Office.

Printed in Great Britain by
Adams Springfield, Sevenoaks, Kent.

Published by Kent County Council,
Planning Department, Springfield,
Maidstone, Kent ME14 2LX.

First published June 1994.

ISBN 1 873 01044 3

CONTENTS

To the best of our knowledge the interpretive content and all other information is believed to be correct. We should be grateful if you would inform us of any changes, omissions or errors, so that modifications can be made in subsequent revisions of the book.

INTRODUCTION

The High Weald Walk has been developed by the Kent High Weald Project in conjunction with the East Sussex Recreation & Countryside Management Service. It forms a 27½ mile circular route through the countryside around Royal Tunbridge Wells and is linked to the centre of the town by four linear routes.

For most of the High Weald Walk, the route follows existing rights of way. These have all been upgraded. New stiles and steps have been erected and new bridges installed where required. Waymarks, with a distinctive logo, show the exact line of the route. The High Weald Walk links at various points with other long-distance paths. The Wealdway, the Sussex Border Path and the Forest Way Country Park all intersect and add to the range of possible routes you may take.

HIGH WEALD

An Area of Outstanding Natural Beauty (AONB)

The High Weald AONB covers an area of about 560 square miles stretching from Horsham in the west to Tenterden and Rye in the east. It was designated under the National Parks and Countryside Act of 1949 and confirmed by the Secretary of State for the Environment in 1983.

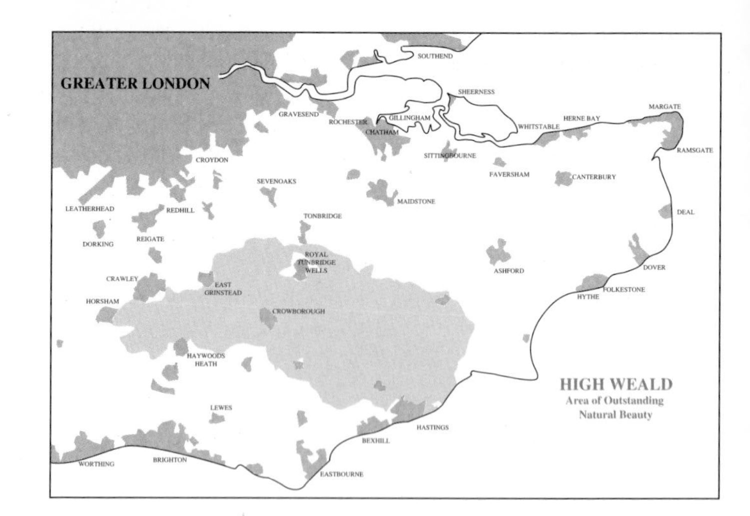

With its patchwork of fields, hedges and woodland, its steep-sided valleys, and its often dramatic views of rolling slopes, the High Weald presents a countryside found nowhere else in the country. Its churches, barns and oast-houses have grown from the nature of the countryside. Its agriculture, industries and settlements are closely linked.

Within the area encompassed by the High Weald Walk, the scenery changes from sandstone ridges to the wooded valleys and ghylls which are such a distinctive feature of the region. Woods and shaws are integral parts of the traditional farmed landscape. The area supports a wide range of wildlife habitats of great importance to our environmental heritage.

The term Weald refers to the whole area between the North and South Downs, including the Greensand ridge. It is derived from Andredswald, the Saxon name for the huge forest (wald) behind the Roman Anderida, now Pevensey, which covered the South East in ancient times.

What is known as the High Weald is the central region, a hilly area with many steep-sided valleys, although nowhere does it rise to a height greater than 200m. To understand the High Weald you must first look at the geology that underpins the landscape, considered by many to be the most interesting in Europe.

Geology

The High Weald strata started forming around 160 million years ago, in Lower Cretaceous times.

At that point the last of the Jurassic rocks were being formed. These were the Purbeck Beds which contain the marble of that name and also bear some iron. For the next 30 million years, the Cretacous period, the area of what was to become the Weald varied between inland swamp and dry savannah, as the climate and the soil level changed.

Tree shaded bank above Groombridge Place

This was the age of reptiles, above all the dinosaurs, with Iguanodon among others roaming here. It was Iguanodon's skeleton, found at Cuckfield in 1830, which helped to date and identify the period. Several rivers flowed into the area bringing sands, grit, stone and clay, depositing them to form either deltas or islands according to their flow. Pressure from later layers helped to solidify them.

In the Lower Cretaceous Wealden layers, you will find five main strata appearing at different points around the High Weald. Their names derive from the area where you see them most clearly.

Immediately above the Purbeck Beds are the layers known as the Hastings Beds. These are comprised of clays, including the iron-bearing Wadhurst Clay, then two distinct layers of Tunbridge Wells Sand, separated by another clay layer. The lower layer of the Tunbridge Wells Sand produces the fine, hard Ardingly sandstone. On top of this lie between 400 to 800 feet of Weald clay.

The weight of the upper layers caused the centre to subside forming a basin into which the sea entered about 120 million years ago. For the next 10 million years marine deposits were laid down, forming the Lower Greensand, the Gault clay and the Upper Greensand layers. Then crustacean deposits settled to form a final chalk layer. In their entirety, the marine deposits eventually rose over 300 metres above the Wealden deposits.

Around 100,000 years BC a period of extensive earth movements, probably connected with those which formed the Alps, pushed the centre of the Weald upwards to a height of 970 metres. The resulting dome, the Wealden anticline, represents the area of the present High Weald. This was subsequently greatly eroded and the present highest point in the High Weald is at Crowborough, Sussex (185m).

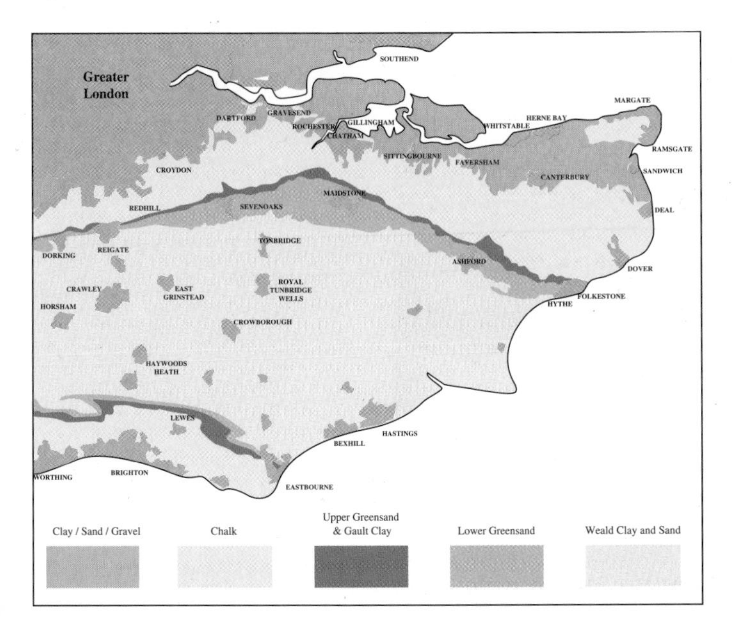

Many new stiles have been erected on the High Weald Walk

Weathering from wind and rain began the process of erosion, gouging out rivers and wearing away weaker formations. The Ice Ages accelerated the process with recurrent cycles of frost and thaw causing the rocks to crack and split. Solifluction, a process whereby a mass of earth slides over harder frozen ground, moved large expanses of ground, whilst rivers cut further into the softer rocks.

When the last ice cap retreated the chalk cover had disintegrated from the centre. The stronger Hastings Beds of the central dome were left heavily ridged and furrowed, with smooth tops and deep-cut ghylls. Around these lay the Wealden clay. Beyond rose the Greensand ridges, then the Downs, their scarp faces the result of the violent movements that distorted and reshaped the area.

Landscape

Here was the beginning of the High Weald landscape as we know it now. Outcrops of the hardest rock, the Ardingly sandstone such as you find at Toad Rock, High Rocks, Eridge Rocks and Harrison's Rocks were now apparent. Four main rivers drained the slopes, including the Medway from the north and the Rother from the south-east.

In some places the relationship between the geological structure and the landscape is clear, with the Tunbridge Wells Sand on the higher ground, the Wadhurst Clay in the valley bottoms. In other places there has been so much faulting and folding that there is no fixed sequence.

The next element, the woodland cover, began to develop from about 8000 BC. Dwarf birch and willow slowly spread northwards from the main mass of the continent, followed later by Scots pine and hazel, oak and elm. A warm, wet period between 5500 and 3000 BC, known as the Atlantic period, saw the arrival of alder and lime in the lowlands of England. After the break-off from the continent, fewer species arrived naturally. Other

Outline Geological Section across the Downs and Weald

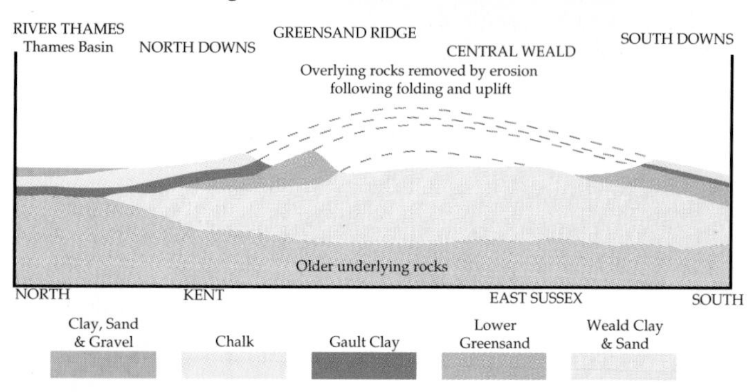

common trees such as spruce, sycamore, apple and chestnut, were introduced by man.

The landscape developed through a close interaction between people and their environment as they used, and in some cases, replenished, the natural resources available.

Woodland Management

Present-day woodlands show both exploitation and management. With the steady removal of wood, initially for firewood, then in Neolithic times through clearance for grazing, pasture and agriculture, the ancient woodlands gradually declined. When Celtic people arrived from Europe around 400 BC, with their ability to make iron tools and stronger ploughs, clearance continued with greater speed. Romans, Romano-British and Anglo-Saxons continued the process and the pattern of woodland settlements beside cultivated or grazed fields became established.

The 14th-century population increase after the Black Death coincided with new technology in iron-making and a greater demand for charcoal. Ship-building, bark for use in the tanning industry and lime extraction increased the rate of clearance.

Traditional woodland management techniques, such as coppicing, practiced to some extent since Neolithic times, not only sustained the surviving woodland but also created much of the woodland pattern we have come to know. This is the method whereby trees, notably hazel and sweet chestnut, are cut down at intervals of between 12 and 20 years. From the stumps new growth is soon established, which in turn provides fresh timber. Widescale coppicing met many of the demands of early industry. Subsequently it provided fencing and hop poles for agriculture.
Another traditional method, pollarding, provided a way to mix pasture and woodland. By lopping branches at two to three metres above ground level, farmers provided winter fodder for their animals and timber for building. Pollarding not only protects trees from pigs and cattle, but can also reinvigorate several species.

Between the 17th and 19th centuries landowners added to the stock of wood available by creating new plantations, mainly of oak, beech, ash and elm. Hazel and sweet chestnut were used for coppice wood. The exotic trees you will see in parkland were introduced during and after the 16th century, as explorers returned from distant travel.

Much of the woodland in this area was severely affected by the storm of 1987. The impact has been to some extent mitigated by a heightened awareness of woodland management.

This, combined with schemes to replant agricultural land and to create amenity woodland, has led to a number of fresh plantings in the area of the High Weald Walk.

Walkers, particularly when accompanied by dogs, should be careful not to disturb livestock

Industry

The geology of the High Weald has given rise to several major industries. These too have helped to shape the landscape.

The iron industry existed from pre-Roman times when Celtic settlers made use of the iron readily available in nodules in the Wadhurst Clay. The plentiful wood supply and good streams of the High Weald were an important attribute. The industry particularly flourished during the Middle Ages and Tudor times, encouraged by the demand for ammunition for war. You will find reminders in names such as Forge Wood and Minepit Wood. The iron industry came to an end when coal was found to do the job more efficiently and more cheaply in Derbyshire.

In early times furnaces, known as bloomeries, usually consisted of a shallow hollow in the ground covered by a clay-walled mound. In this, ore was roasted on charcoal fanned by bellows. The result was a spongy form of wrought iron which could then be hammered into shape by the smith at his forge. In the 13th and 14th centuries output almost trebled, as people learned to harness water to power the bellows.

In Tudor times the blast furnace was introduced from the continent. A stronger blast of air created a temperature high enough to liquefy the ore to produce cast iron. The chief product was cannon and shot. Firebacks and railings were also popular products.

Lime, found in the Purbeck Beds and in parts of the Wadhurst Clay, was used in the 17th and early-18th centuries for agriculture and for building. Clay was regularly used for brick and tile-making. Sandstone also provided excellent building material.

The High Weald is traditionally an area of mixed farming

Horticulture and Agriculture

Unlike the Low Weald, where alluvial silt has added to the fertility of the soil, the soils of the High Weald have always been relatively poor, with sandy loam and sandy clays. Grazing and pasture have played an important part from the earliest times. The High Weald has subsequently been an area of mixed farming, producing hops, top fruit, (apples, pears, cherries and plums) and cereals such as winter wheat. From the late 1970s the mixed pattern has been in decline and many changes are now apparent.

You will still occasionally find orchards of the traditional size, often no more than 15-20 acres, interspersed with lines of wind-breaks, these usually being poplars. However, the majority of old orchards have disappeared. The taller, 'standard' fruit trees are yielding to closely packed 'bush' varieties, and you will seldom now see inter-cropping and grazing. Tunbridge Wells Sand is, in general, well-suited to top fruit since it is free-draining, with open slopes normally free from frost. With dwarfing rootstock appropriate to the soil, farmers can produce fruit that meets the exacting requirements of present-day marketing.

Hops have been a well-known feature of the Kent and Sussex countryside since they were introduced from the Low Countries at the end of the 15th century. Opposed at first by many people as 'an unwholesome weed' which adulterated good ale, hops nevertheless became popular for the flavour they give beer and for their preservative qualities. Kent became the earliest centre of hop growing, not only because of its proximity to the Netherlands but also because of its closed field system of farming, its suitable soils and its good supply of wood for charcoal and hop poles. Now the County supports two-thirds of the industry.

Hop growing reached a peak in the late-19th century when more than 70,000 acres were cultivated. In this century the demand for hops has declined, mainly through competition from the USA, Europe and even China. A further problem is wilt, though research at Wye College in Kent has developed a number of wilt resistant types.

Though some mechanisation has entered hop-growing, it is still highly labour-intensive, as you will see if you watch stringing in the spring, twiddling in the summer or harvesting in the autumn.

Arable farming is also changing. In the past you would see many small farms working less than

Grazing pasture, a significant land use in the High Weald

100 acres, with small cereal-producing fields of no more than 17 acres to a crop.

Today, a cereal farmer needs 400 acres to make a living, and often combines with other farmers to work an area. Where smaller farms continue you will find pasture and grazing now predominates. Diversification and changing economic circumstances has seen many oast-houses and barns converted to dwellings, studios and workshops.

Natural History

The natural history of the High Weald has been strongly influenced by man's interaction with his environment. A finely balanced relationship developed between nature and farming, forestry and industrial practices.

Woodland still remains the dominant habitat. In ancient woods, where trees can be traced back to at least AD 1600, you will find undisturbed soil with species such as birch, oak and hazel. Smaller shaws, often remnants of ancient woodland, provide connecting routes between these larger blocks. Most of these support the characteristic woodland fauna and flora.

The steeply incised wooded valleys running down from the High Weald, known as ghylls, are particularly important. Their stable, moist micro-climate supports ferns and bryophites (mosses and lichens). They often perpetuate conditions from the warm Atlantic period of 4000 BC and sustain flora from the forests of that time, more commonly found in the wetter west of Britain.

Coppice woodland supports a variety of wildlife, especially in its early stages, and pollarded trees encourage a rich invertebrate life. Heathland has existed probably from Mesolithic times, when clearances left a poor sandy soil structure. The Ashdown Forest to the west is the largest remaining area of lowland heath in the area, but you will also find some fragments on Tunbridge Wells Common and at Pembury Walks. Heathland provides a habitat for a variety of rare birds and animals, reptiles and invertebrates.

Grassland now covers over half of the High Weald. Much of it is poor in species through 'improvement' by fertiliser and through long-term over-grazing. There are very few areas of unimproved meadow, but where they exist, such as at Danemore Park, you will find a diverse range of wildflowers and grasses.

The sandstone outcrops offer another rare habitat. The porous rock above impervious clay retains moisture. Where there is also a woodland canopy this creates a humid, frost-free micro-climate which supports more of the 'Atlantic' species.

Arable land is generally poor in wildlife species, but you can find valuable habitats in field corners, wet areas and headlands, where there may be incentives to avoid spraying.

Other important species-rich habitats in the High Weald include hedgerows and road verges. Churchyards managed for wildlife often develop strong communities of bryophites (lichens and mosses). The High Weald also has a high concentration of ponds, many of which are the result of human activity such as mining and marling. Others existed as hammer ponds for the iron industry. Abandoned quarries are another useful habitat.

Human Settlement, Archaeology and History

Evidence of the earliest inhabitants of the High Weald, Mesolithic (Middle Stone Age, 4500 BC) and Neolithic man, has been found at High Rocks on the Kent-Sussex border. Celts, who arrived in England from 500 BC, settled at High Rocks around 200-100 BC. They also settled at two other high points, Castle Hill and Saxonbury, where remains of their iron-working and pottery have been unearthed dating from the second century BC.

The lych-gate at St Alban's Church has an unusual weather vane set into its hexagonal ceiling

Clearance of the Wealden forest, as people sought pasture, grazing and arable land, took far longer in the remote region of the High Weald than on the more fertile Greensand ridges and the downs to the north and south. At the time Domesday Book was drawn up, in 1086, only a small fraction of the population settled here, nearer, on average, one person to every two miles rather than up to around 15 to one mile by the channel coast.

In the immediate area of the High Weald Walk you will find only Tonbridge (Tonebrige) and Tudeley (Tuidele) mentioned in that survey.

But Domesday Book only referred to civil, not ecclesiastical matters. Although not mentioned, churches and parishes also existed, and we hear of Speldhurst and Pembury, among others, in records of the time. Small settlements such as Frant and Southborough had long been growing, on common land on the edge of the great feudal forests, South Frith and Waterdown, or in other clearings where the ground was favourable.

From Norman times onwards, men exerted increasing influence on the environment. The population doubled between the writing of Domesday Book in 1086 and the Black Death (1348-50), so increasing woodland clearance. Land ownership played an increasing part. At first this was in the hands of the state, while the church had its own jurisdiction. Then, as church and state each pulled its own way, and as individuals and their families prospered or declined, land changed hands at an increasing rate. Smaller parcels were sold from each estate, more buildings erected on them.

The parish system had existed since Saxon times. Within their boundaries, manors such as Rusthall and Groombridge flourished in their own right. Groombridge even had a small chapel on the land. But these were still part of a much larger ecclesiastical unit. Only in the 19th century, as communications developed and population grew, did most of these small communities acquire their own parish and their own church.

enabled Tunbridge Wells to expand further

Royal Tunbridge Wells itself, now a focal point in this part of the High Weald, was a late arrival, developing from the 17th century.

In 1609 Lord North, returning from the Abergavenny estate at Eridge, discovered one of the many small springs whose water had health-giving properties. His chance find led thousands more to come and take the water at the Wells.

The Local Government Act of 1894 re-aligned many parishes to become more manageable units. In April 1974, under the Local Government Act of 1972, Tunbridge Wells District Council was set up. Now Tunbridge Wells Borough Council, it covers all the Kent villages of the Walk. Wealden District Council of East Sussex covers the villages of Frant, Eridge Green and the Sussex section of Groombridge.

Roads and Railways

Communications developed in response to the population and added to its growth. The A21, the main route from London to Hastings, became a Turnpike Road in 1709, and provided the first main route to Tunbridge Wells from Woodsgate, near Pembury. The prehistoric route later used by the Romans, from Oldbury, through Tonbridge, Southborough and Frant, was Turnpiked in 1765. In the mid-19th century the railway, widely welcomed, opened the area to further expansion.

The lake at Somerhill, one of several historic parklands on the High Weald Walk

HIGH WEALD WALK LOGO

The design of the High Weald Walk logo is adapted from that used by the Kent High Weald Project.

WALKING ADVICE

No season of the year is closed to walkers; enjoyment can be gained from walking on a bright crisp winter's morning, or on an 'Indian summer's day' in the autumn. Equally rewarding is a springtime walk when the countryside is full of new life and growth.

Always wear suitable clothing and footwear for the season. Be prepared for changeable weather. Take with you clothes which are warm and waterproof. Inexpensive overtrousers will protect you from any discomfort caused by walking through high

Ponds are an important feature of the High Weald landscape

vegetation or crops after rain. Sections of the path may be muddy after periods of rain so wear strong, comfortable and waterproof footwear.

Allow plenty of time to complete your chosen walk. Reckon on walking 2 or $2\frac{1}{2}$ miles an hour. The distances and times for each section of the walk are shown on the route maps, and in the information. Allow more time if it has been wet, if you are elderly, or have children or inexperienced walkers with you.

The route has been established in consultation with landowners and farmers and follows public rights of way and permissive paths. Remember that most public paths cross private estates and farmland; they were developed as routes from farms to the nearest village, and were not designed for large numbers of people. You are walking through a place of work; enjoy the countryside but please show respect for its life and work. Crops and animals are the farmers' livelihood, so they should be left undisturbed.

Always keep to the path to avoid trespass. When faced with a growing crop you may have to seek a way around the edge of the field even though in law the landowner or farmer is supposed to keep the footpath clear. Walk in single file through a crop. In case you come across a path which has become overgrown, you will find it useful to carry secateurs to help clear the way. You may remove any obstruction on a right of way sufficiently to allow you to proceed. Take care when crossing or walking along country roads. Keep to the right, in single file, facing oncoming traffic. On a bend, however, walk on the outside and keep a good lookout for traffic.

Remember to leave things as they are - refasten those gates you find closed. Straying stock can cause damage and an expensive inconvenience to farmers. Always use gates and stiles to cross fences and hedges.

Take your litter home with you otherwise it can injure people, animals and wildlife. Guard against all risk of fire, especially in dry weather. Picnicking is not permitted on private land; you only have a right of passage on a right of way.

To avoid injury or distress to farm animals and wildlife, keep your dogs under control at all times. If not on a lead they can run surprisingly long distances and consequently out of sight of the owner. Please keep your dogs on leads, particularly when passing through fruit growing areas or fields with standing crops. Farmers have a right to shoot dogs found worrying animals.

USING THE GUIDEBOOK

This book is designed to be a practical guide to walking the High Weald Walk in either direction. The route maps have been arranged in sequence in seven sections, from Bullingstone, three miles north-west of Royal Tunbridge Wells. When walking in a clockwise direction, the book is used in a conventional way, whilst the anti-clockwise route is read from section 7 of the book back to the front. Sections 8 to 11 cover the four link routes into Royal Tunbridge Wells.

By carefully folding it back, the book will fit into a map case, thus providing protection against damage, dirt and dampness.

Because the countryside is constantly changing, with stiles, gates and field boundaries being removed or new ones erected, there are no route directions. Route finding should not

Traditional weatherboarded Wealden house

be a problem given the large scale route maps and the extensive waymarking and signing on the ground.

Route Map Information

The route maps are reproduced from the Ordnance Survey Pathfinder Series enlarged to a scale of $3^{1}/_{2}$" to 1 mile (5.5cm to 1km).

The maps are aligned north/south on each page, and the scale appears on each map spread.

Information boards showing a map of the High Weald Walk with text and illustrations interpreting local features are sited at various locations around the route.

Maps

Ordnance Survey sheet numbers and titles.

Landranger Series,
scale 1:50,000 - $1^{1}/_{4}$" to 1 mile
188 Maidstone and The Weald of Kent

Pathfinder Series,
scale 1:25,000 - $2^{1}/_{2}$" to 1 mile
1228 (TQ 44/54) Tonbridge and Edenbridge
1229 (TQ 64/74) Paddock Wood and Staplehurst
1249 (TQ 63/73) Wadhurst, Cranbrook and Bewl Bridge Reservoir
1248 (TQ 43/53) Royal Tunbridge Wells and Forest Row

Distances and Time

The distances and times for each section of the walk are shown on the map spreads and in the information below.

The distances in this guidebook are given in miles. The exact conversion of miles to kilometres is 1 mile to 1.6093km. For convenience the approximate conversion is 1 mile to 1.6km.

Conversion Table

1 mile	=	1.6km
2 miles	=	3.2km
5 miles	=	8.0km
10 miles	=	16.1km

Grid References

The framework of squares spaced at one kilometre intervals over all Ordnance Survey maps is known as the National Grid. The grid facilitates the pinpointing of any place in the country, giving it a unique reference number.

To give a reference number, first take the western (left-hand) edge of the kilometre square in which the place lies. Read the figures at the end of the line in the top and bottom margins of the map, then moving eastwards (to the right) estimate the position of the place in tenths across the square. Secondly, take the southern edge of the same square and read the figures at the end of the line in the side margins of the map. Then, moving northwards, estimate the position of the place in tenths up the square. This gives the place a six figure reference number accurate to within 100 metres.

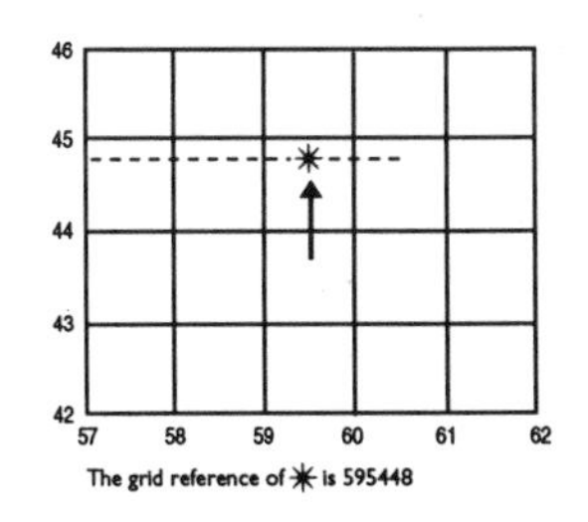

The grid reference of ✳ is 595448

In finding out a grid reference, the first three numbers of the six figure number refer to the line and number of tenths across the square, whilst the second three numbers refer to the line and number of tenths up the square. The grid references of interesting features on or near the route of the High Weald Walk are given in the narrative text.

Planning a Walk

The High Weald Walk is $27^{1}/_{2}$ miles in length and can be undertaken as a long distance walk in one or more days, using the main and/or link routes. A series of shorter walks, using a combination of the waymarked link and main routes, cater for the family group or casual walker.

If you wish to undertake the High Weald Walk in sections you need to be aware of problems of returning to your starting point. Possible solutions might be as follows:

a) Using two cars, one at the starting point and the other at the proposed finishing point;

b) Using one car and public transport. If relying on infrequent bus services it is suggested that you make your

Abergavenny monograms adorn cottages in and around Eridge Green

outward journey by bus thus returning confidently to your car or base;

c) Retracing your steps - the scenery can look surprisingly different when you are walking the other way.

The walk can be undertaken as a whole or in sections, with the following suggested itineraries:

One day marathon
27½ miles, allow 11/12 hours.

Two days
approximately 14 miles each, allow 6/7 hours.

Three days
approximately 9 miles each, allow 4/5 hours.

You can devise shorter walks using the bus routes which radiate from Royal Tunbridge Wells and link with the following places along the route: Speldhurst, Southborough, Five Oak Green Road (via Tonbridge), Pembury, Kent and Sussex Crematorium, Frant, Eridge Green, Groombridge, Junction of A264 and B2188.

The High Weald Walk logo, identifies the route for walkers

Lakes in Eridge Park, once pen ponds for the nearby forge and furnace

Circular Walks
The following circular walks can be undertaken either way using the link routes along the High Weald Walk:

High Brooms Station (bus or train to or from Royal Tunbridge Wells) - Railway Viaduct (Old Forge Farm) - High Wood - Mount Sion (Royal Tunbridge Wells)
13 miles, allow 5/6 hours

Mount Sion (Royal Tunbridge Wells) - High Wood - Groombridge - Tunbridge Wells Common.
15 miles, allow 6/7 hours

Tunbridge Wells Common - Groombridge - Speldhurst - Tunbridge Wells Common.
10 miles, allow 4/5 hours

Tunbridge Wells Common - Speldhurst - Railway Viaduct - High Brooms Station (bus or train to or from Royal Tunbridge Wells).
8¼ miles, allow 3/4 hours

WAYMARKING AND SIGNING

Introduction
The term waymarking refers to marking objects along a public right of way. It complements signposting, which shows where a right of way leaves the metalled road and indicates its initial direction, and enables users to follow a path accurately and confidently at points where they might otherwise have difficulty.

Waymarking benefits not only users of rights of way but also farmers and landowners. It increases users' enjoyment of the countryside and helps to prevent unintentional trespass.

The Waymarking System
The recommended system in England and Wales uses small coloured arrows to show the direction of the path and also to act as a target when viewed from a distance. A different colour is used for each category of right of way:

- public rights of way that are footpaths are waymarked using yellow arrows;
- bridleways are waymarked with blue arrows;
- byways open to all traffic and other routes that may legally be used by wheeled vehicles are waymarked with red arrows, but they are intended only to show the status of the route and not to indicate whether it is physically suitable for vehicles.

If the status of a path changes along its length, so does the colour of the waymarking arrows. Where a right of way is part of a special route, such as a National Trail, Recreation Route or circular walk, the arrows are used in conjunction with the route's own symbol.

High Weald Walk
The High Weald Walk logos are used to show the line of the route in the countryside. You will see them inset on to waymark posts, or posts of gates or stiles. The Walk has been waymarked in such a way that it is possible for you to walk the route in either direction. The High Weald Walk logo is incorporated with the different coloured arrows depending on the status of the right of way. The link routes are waymarked with similar coloured arrows with the words LINK ROUTE printed on the logo.

Changes to the route may occur during the currency of this guidebook, in which case look out for the diversion signs and follow the waymarks.

Wherever the High Weald Walk crosses or leaves a metalled road in Kent you will see metal signs fixed to lamp posts or other posts. The logo is added to statutory footpath, bridleway or byway signs, or used on its own where the route follows a section of road.

In East Sussex, wooden sign posts are used at these locations.

The link routes are signed similarly with the words LINK ROUTE added to the sign.

TRANSPORT

Car Parking

Car parking places are shown on the route maps. Please note that these are not necessarily car parks. If a car park is not available, please park thoughtfully and sensibly to avoid causing an obstruction or damage to the roadside verges. Leave your car securely locked with valuables out of sight.

Cuckoo-flower or Lady's Smock (K Rennells)

Old hornbeam marking a field boundary (R Dealler)

Bus and Train Services

It is not practical to give details of all the bus and train routes and services to and along the High Weald Walk, since they may change during the currency of this guidebook. Kent County Council and East Sussex County Council publish annual public transport maps and guides which contain comprehensive bus and rail route maps and lists of bus services and operators (see below).

For details of train services please telephone either Tonbridge (0732) 770111 or London 071-928 5100.

You are advised to check details of your journey before travelling, particularly with respect to Sunday services. Public transport information can be obtained from Kent County Council, Highways and Transportation Department, Springfield, Maidstone, Kent ME14 2LX, ☎ Maidstone (0622) 696996, or East Sussex County Council, Highways and Transportation Department, Sackville House, Brooks Close, Lewes, East Sussex BN7 1UE, ☎ Lewes (0273) 474747 (If calling from Bexhill, Battle, Hastings or Rye, ☎ (0797) 223053).

USEFUL ADDRESSES AND/ OR TELEPHONE NUMBERS

(Please note that all area telephone codes change on 16 April 1995).

If you have any comments or suggestions about this or any other recreation route in Kent, please contact the Access and Recreation Officer, Planning Department, Kent County Council, Springfield, Maidstone, Kent ME14 2LX, ☎ Maidstone (0622) 696168.

In East Sussex, details of countryside sites with public access, or other recreational paths in the County can be obtained from the Access Project, Recreation and Countryside Management Service, East Sussex County Council, Southover House, Southover Road, Lewes, East Sussex BN7 1YA, ☎ Lewes (0273) 481654.

The routes should not be obstructed in any way but if they are in Kent, please contact the Public Rights of Way Manager, Highways & Transportation Department, Kent County Council, Springfield, Maidstone, Kent ME14 2LX, ☎ Maidstone (0622) 696740, or in East Sussex, the High Weald Conservation Project, Recreation and Countryside Management Service, East Sussex County Council, Southover House, Southover Road, Lewes, East Sussex BN7 1YA, ☎ Lewes (0273) 481637.

Tourist Information

(including accommodation lists)

Royal Tunbridge Wells: Tourist Information Centre, The Old

Fishmarket, The Pantiles, Royal Tunbridge Wells, Kent TN2 5TN, ☎ Royal Tunbridge Wells (0892) 515675.

Tonbridge: Tourist Information Centre, Tonbridge Castle, Castle Street, Tonbridge, Kent TN9 1BG, ☎ Tonbridge (0732) 770929.

Boship Roundabout (A22): Tourist Information Centre, Lower Dicker, Hailsham East Sussex BN27 4DP, ☎ (0323) 442667.

Hailsham: Tourist Information Centre, The Library, Western Road, Hailsham, East Sussex B27 3DN, ☎ (0323) 840604

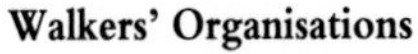

Walkers' Organisations

Ramblers' Association, 1/5 Wandsworth Road, London SW8 2XX, ☎ London 071-582 6878
Kent Area Secretary: Brian Arguile, 42 Waldron Drive, Loose, Maidstone, Kent ME15 9TH, ☎ Maidstone (0622) 744207.
East Sussex Area Secretary: Ross Urquhart, Rock Farm, Potters Mill Lane, Broad Oak, Heathfield, East Sussex TN21 8TX, ☎ Heathfield (0435) 866552.

Long Distance Walkers' Association Secretary: Brian Smith, 10 Temple Park Close, Leeds, West Yorkshire LS15 0JJ, ☎ Leeds (0532) 642205
Kent Area Secretary: Mr D Sheldrake, 26 Highview, Vigo Village, Meopham, Gravesend, Kent DA13 0RR, ☎ Fairseat (0732) 823643.
Sussex Area Secretary: Mr A Carter, ☎ Eastbourne (0323) 726212.

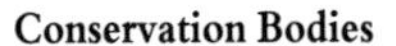

Conservation Bodies

Kent High Weald Project, Council Offices, High Street, Cranbrook, Kent TN17 3EN, ☎ Cranbrook (0580) 712771.

High Weald Conservation Project, Recreation and Countryside Management Service, Southover House, Southover Road, Lewes, East Sussex BN7 1YA, ☎ Lewes (0273) 481637.

Miscellaneous

Ordnance Survey, Romsey Road, Maybush, Southampton, Hants SO9 4DH, ☎ Southampton (0703) 792000.
Weatherdial (up-to-date weather forecast)
Inland Kent 0898 14 12 12
Inland Sussex 0898 14 12 11

St Peter's Church, as viewed from Camden Park

P & R Publicity Ltd (Achievement Badges for most long distance paths), Queensway, Stem Lane Industrial Estate, New Milton, Hants BH25 5NN.

ACCOMMODATION

Bed and breakfast establishments are located in the following places: Royal Tunbridge Wells, Southborough, Tonbridge (1 mile) Pembury (1/3 mile), Hawkenbury (link route), Frant, Eridge (1 mile), Groombridge, Langton Green (1/2 mile), Modest Corner, Rusthall (link route).

Please telephone the Tourist Information Centres (listed on page 14) for details.

For a copy of the Kent Accommodation Guide, contact Kent Tourism, Economic Development Department, Kent County Council, Springfield, Maidstone, Kent ME14 2LX, ☎ Maidstone (0622) 696165.
For a copy of the East Sussex Accommodation Guide, contact Economic Development, Planning Department, East Sussex County Council, Southover House, Southover Road, Lewes, East Sussex, BN7 1YA, ☎ Lewes (0273) 481886.

The Ramblers' Association (also listed) publishes the Ramblers' Year Book and Accommodation Guide. The book is available from local bookshops.

Youth Hostels Association, Trevelyan House, 8 St Stephens Hill, St Albans, Herts AL1 2DY, ☎ St Albans (0727) 55215.

Friezland Wood, owned by the Woodland Trust (K Rennells)

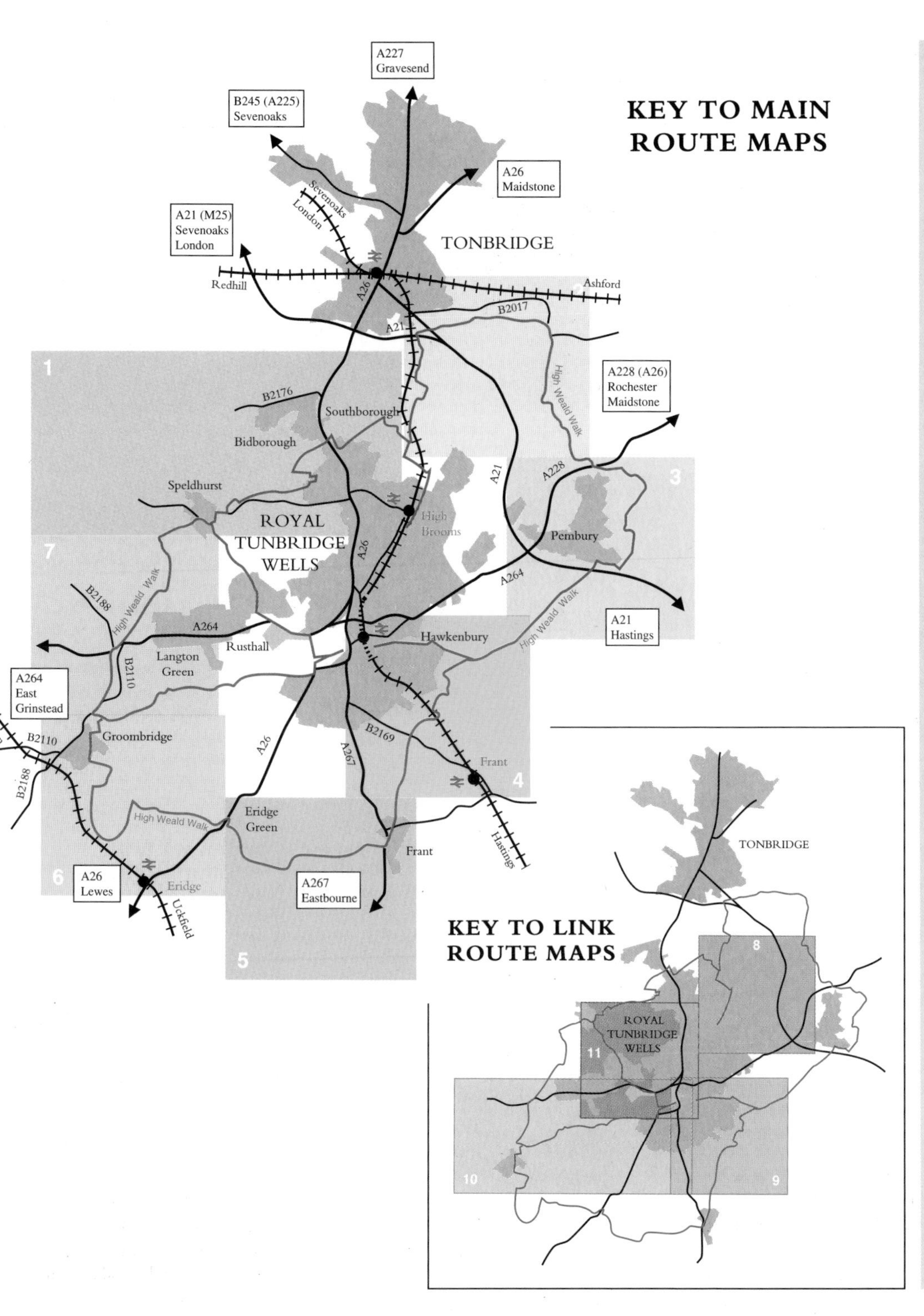

KEY TO MAP SYMBOLS

- High Weald Walk - fully signed and waymarked
- Link route (access point) - fully signed and waymarked
- Other footpaths - not promoted
- **WT65** Right of Way number
- **42** Ordnance Survey grid number
- 26 Interesting feature
- 26 Miles from Southborough Common (clockwise)
- Railway station
- Bus route
- Car parking
- Telephone
- Tourist Information
- Toilet
- Accommodation
- Public house
- Pub food
- Cafe/restaurant
- Refreshments
- Picnic site
- Foodstore
- Farm shop
- View point
- Caution - take care

1 Bullingstone - Southborough Valley

4¼ miles - allow 2¼ hours

Bullingstone

For many centuries, the High Weald has preserved its dense woodland cover, far longer in fact than the lower parts of Kent and Sussex. However by 1218, a farmer, Baluinch, had settled on some isolated slopes above the River Medway, grazing his animals and ploughing some land. The clearing became known as Baluinch-stane (homestead). Today Bullingstone (1) (TQ 544413) remains apart, an attractive row of 15th-century houses stretched along Bullingstone Lane. To the south lies Burnt Wood, with the characteristic slopes of a typical, steep-sided Wealden ghyll. To the north-east the ground rises more slowly to give fine views over the River Medway (2) (TQ 532417) and the western Weald.

Speldhurst

The village of Speldhurst (3) (TQ 554414), is the oldest parish in this part of the High Weald, with records going back to at least 1239. Until the 19th century many of the adjoining villages, such as Rusthall, Groombridge and Langton Green, each now with its own church, were simply manors within Speldhurst.

A number of attractive cottages line Bullingstone Lane

A Church of St Mary the Virgin (3) (TQ 554414) has stood at the centre of Speldhurst since Saxon days, but the building has been rebuilt several times. Over the porch you will see a coat of arms charged with the fleur-de-lys and bearing the label of a French Royal Duke.

This commemorates Charles Duc d'Orleans who was captured at Agincourt in 1415 and held prisoner for 25 years by Sir Richard Waller of Groombridge. He gave money which should have gone to pay his ransom to help refurbish the church. That church was struck by lightning at the end of the 18th century. The next succumbed to dry rot within a century.

The present church, built in 1871, faithfully reproduces the designs and dimensions of the medieval church it replaced. You can see the architect's attention to detail throughout. The stained glass windows form an outstanding collection of 19th-century work by the pre-Raphaelites, Edward Burne-Jones and William Morris, and by the Sussex artist, Charles Kempe. In these windows you will see clearly the pre-Raphaelite aim to depict realism and emotion and to return to medieval styles. You will also see Morris' use of nature for decoration.

Church of St Mary the Virgin, Speldhurst

The cemetery, which contains a number of tombstones of considerable architectural interest, is also important for its wildlife. Both on the acid soil as well as on the walls and tombs you will find a wide range of mosses and lichens, some of them more commonly seen in the north and west of Britain.

The 'George and Dragon' (6) (TQ 554414) is thought to have been built in 1212. Tradition tells that Kentish bowmen of the place revelled there after the battle of Agincourt in 1415. Tunnels thought to run under ground to the church may have been used by some of the many smugglers who operated in Kent and Sussex in the 17th century.

Beside the stream in the valley below Speldhurst you will see one of the best surviving examples of a 19th-century water mill (7) (TQ 558417). Corn production was at its height in the Weald at this time but most mills in this region have now gone.

Broomhill

Out of site, on the slope to the south lies Broomhill (8) (TQ 568416) built in 1852 for Sir David Salomons Bt. (1793-1873). He was a financier, a prominent leader of the Anglo-Jewish emancipation movement, and the first Jew to become a Sheriff, Alderman and Lord Mayor of London. The architect was Decimus Burton, especially known for his design of Hyde Park corner and of Calverley Park in Tunbridge Wells.

Salomons' nephew, Sir David Lionel Salomons, built the brick tower, now a water tower (9) (TQ 569417), with battlements, and a small staircase turret at one corner, to hold a celestial telescope.

Sir David Lionel Salomons was a pioneer in various fields. He installed electricity in his house as early as 1882, then introduced it into the town when Mayor of Tunbridge Wells in 1894. He organised England's first Motor Show, the Horseless Carriage Exhibition, in 1895. You can see his collection of cars in the stables he built in 1890. A Science Theatre, built in 1894, is now used for regular musical festivals and is renowned for its excellent acoustics.

In the hollow below Constitution Hill (TQ 575423) you will find a small, damp ravine typical of many in the High Weald. The water which emerges from a spring (10) (TQ 573423) between the sandstone and the impermeable clay, contains the iron and other health-giving minerals which made the area famous when Lord North discovered the Wells in 1606. The name 'chalybeate', shown on the map at several of these sites, comes from the Chalybes, a people from the Black Sea coast of Turkey, who were among the first to work iron.

Southborough Common

Southborough Common (12) (TQ 574426) has been formed by the interaction of man and nature. It offers a fascinating mixture of landscape and social history. From Norman times onwards it lay within the lowy or domain of Tonbridge Castle. Nearby to the east lay the vast hunting forest of South Frith. Covering between 500 and 600 acres and stretching from Tonbridge to what was to become Mount Sion in Tunbridge Wells, it was maintained by its owners purely for hunting. Small communities

Holden Pond, once heavily polluted, is now a wildlife haven cared for by local residents

developed outside the forest's boundaries and enjoyed the rights allowed on common land such as sand-digging, turf-cutting, fishing, grazing and fence-making.

Modest Corner (11) (TQ 571424) was one of these communities. Its name may come from John Mode of Tonbridge who lived there in the early-14th century. When Tunbridge Wells became a spa town, a camp was set up at Modest Corner for the visitors. Some claim that their immoderate behaviour led to the current name.

Southborough Common has always been a centre of industry. In the early-19th century, three mills stood in this area. Two, at Bentham Farm (13) (TQ 569424), were water mills, known as the morning and the afternoon mill, and used accordingly to conserve the water supply. The third, a windmill built in 1789 but destroyed in a gale in the 1820s, stood at Mill Platt (14) (TQ 576423). The mills account for the many paths on the common, trodden by farmers as they went to and fro with sacks of grain or flour. Another early-19th century industry, tanning, created great nuisance from the smell and pollution it caused.

Holden Pond (14) (TQ 574423) was once heavily polluted by effluent from this tannery. Now you will see good plant life around its edges, with hovering dragonflies. Like the 95 acres of the common, the pond now forms part of a Site of Nature Conservation Interest.

During the late-18th and 19th century the population increased rapidly. More and larger houses were built. St Peter's Church (19) (TQ 577427) was built in 1830 by Decimus Burton for a congregation of 500. It was enlarged in 1883, when the steeple was introduced.

Southborough has historic links with the game of cricket. It has been played on Southborough Green (20) (TQ 576428) since the late-18th century. Furthermore, the manufacture of cricket balls constituted one of Southborough's two main industries in the 19th and early-20th centuries. The other was brick-making. The heading

Cricket has been played on Southborough Green for two centuries

on the coat of arms, granted in 1953, shows a cricket ball flanked by two bricks.

INTERESTING FEATURES

1 Bullingstone

Bullingstone is a small hamlet, with an attractive row of 15th-century houses stretched along Bullingstone Lane. The first recorded settler here was Baluinch, in the 13th century.

2 River Medway

The 'sweet river' to the Celts who first named it, rises as a spring from the Tunbridge Wells Sands in Ashdown Forest above Turner's Hill near East Grinstead. It drains the northern slopes of the High Weald, acting as a catchment river for the many smaller streams which run off the impermeable clay slopes. A flood storage area above Tonbridge controls the serious flooding which occurs downstream in times of heavy rainfall.

3 Speldhurst

Speldhurst is the oldest parish in this area, with a recorded history dating back to the 13th century.

Church of St Mary the Virgin

This church is little over a century old. It contains some remains of the 14th-century building and has a fine collection of stained glass windows. The churchyard provides a habitat for many mosses and lichens unusual in this area.

4 Speldhurst Rectory

The rectory was originally a glebe house. Some parts may be nearly 800 years old.

5 The Manor House

The sandstone manor house was built in the mid-19th century. Robert Baden-Powell, a relation of the owner, and whose family lived at Langton Green, wrote 'Scouting for Boys' while staying here and established a group of scouts in the parish.

Sheep have been an important part of the Wealden rural economy for hundreds of years

Ancient woodland on Southborough Common – Winter

The Beehive Public House, a short detour off the route at Modest Corner

6 'George and Dragon'
The 'George and Dragon' was once a coaching inn, said to have been the scene for celebration after the battle of Agincourt in 1415. It has been a public house for 200 years.

7 Water Mill
The wheel of Speldhurst Mill is almost 12 feet in diameter. It was driven as water pushed iron buckets which hung from it.

8 Broomhill
Broomhill is a 19th-century country house built by Decimus Burton. The first owner, Sir David Salomons, was a prominent leader of the Jewish Emancipation Movement.

9 Water Tower
This tower was built by his nephew, Sir David Lionel Salomons, to hold a celestial telescope.

10 The Chalybeate Spring
The spring is one of the many which appear at the junction of the Tunbridge Wells Sand and the Wadhurst Clay. The high iron content is considered to have curative properties.

11 Modest Corner
Modest Corner was the site of an early community living beside the common. Woods Cottage and The Old Cottage were among the original buildings here. The Beehive Public House was converted from two farm-houses into a brewery in 1857, and first licensed in 1873.

12 Southborough Common
The common was once grazing land on the edge of the South Frith forest. Its rich wildlife includes over 60 species of birds and many butterflies and moths.

13 Bentham Farmhouse
This farmhouse was built in the 17th century, with traditional hung-tiles. Two watermills stood here in the early-19th century.

14 Mill Platt
Mill Platt was the site of a windmill built in 1789 by John Weaver. After it collapsed in a storm it was replaced by a stream-driven mills.

SPELDHURST

Cock Pit Wood

Bullingstone

Wealdway

Link Route 4 *see page* 50

Holden Corner
Once the site of another early community, Holden Corner was one of the first areas to witness the building of more substantial dwellings.

15 Holden House
Built in 1749, this was one of the first larger houses to be built as the population increased.

Holden Cottage
This cottage was built by Henry Crundwell, owner of the nearby tannery, in 1809.

16 Tanyard Lane and Crundwell Road
These roads recall the days when a tannery lay immediately to the east. Owned by the Crundwell family for over a century, some of the leather was used for cricket balls.

17 Pumping station
Built on the site of the public pump in 1885, the pumping station enabled a steady supply of fresh water to reach local inhabitants.

18 Cat's Castle
Otherwise known as Grove Lodge, with brick ground floor and weatherboarding, this house was originally built in accordance with an old custom. This allowed that the owner could claim possession of the land if he built a house between sundown and sunrise, and had smoke rising from the chimney by dawn.

19 St Peter's Church
This church was first built by Decimus Burton in 1830. It acquired its unusual spire when it was enlarged in 1883.

20 Southborough Green
Cricket has been played here for two centuries. Its first officially recorded match took place in 1838.

Route of the A26
A route has been used along the line of the A26 since prehistoric times. It was created a turnpike road by Act of Parliament in 1765.

'Hand and Sceptre'
This public house, much frequented by cricketers, was built in 1663. It became an inn in 1728.

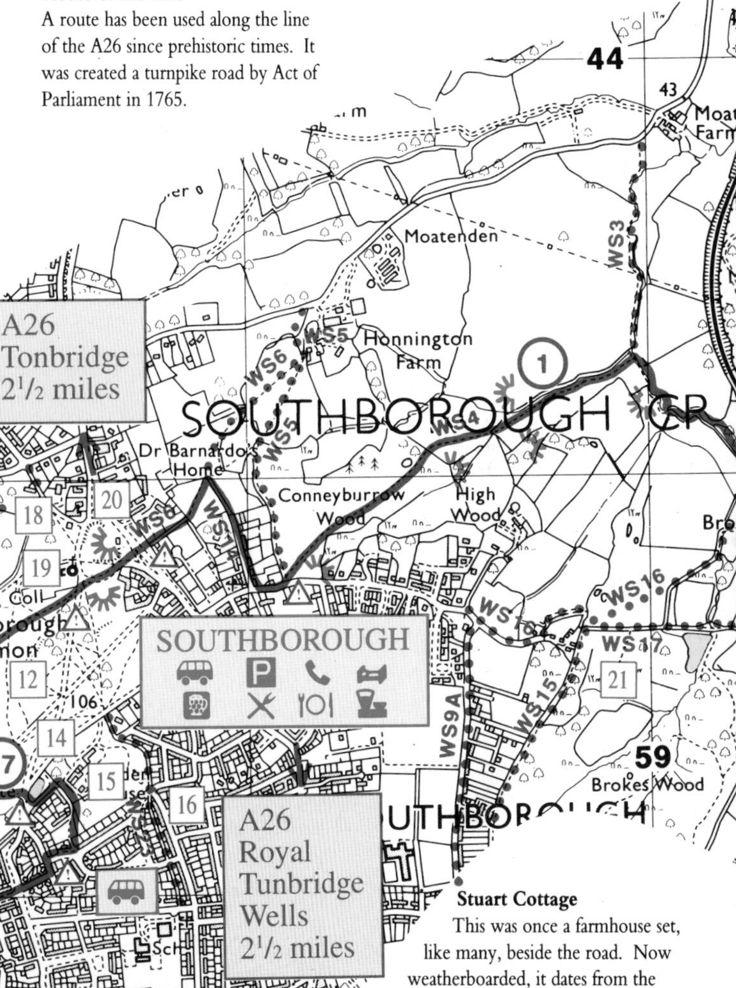

Stuart Cottage
This was once a farmhouse set, like many, beside the road. Now weatherboarded, it dates from the 16th century.

21 Ivy House Farm
A Wealden hall house, built in the early-15th century, this the oldest house in the area. It was once owned by an ironmaster, John Kipping, who was Constable of this part of Tonbridge.

2 Southborough Valley - Old Pembury

$5^1/_2$ miles - allow $2^3/_4$ hours

Southborough Valley
In the late Middle Ages, the Southborough valley was a centre of industrial activity. The stream provided power for several iron works. Iron blooms from ore in the Wadhurst Clay nearby were smelted at Vauxhall Furnace (25) (TQ 592440), then transported to the Old Forge at Brokes Mill, Southborough, (22) (TQ 593428) where they would be hammered into firebacks and other implements. These works were closed in the 17th century, the forge cinder finally dispersed with the building of the viaduct (23) (TQ 594428) in 1845. Names and buildings in the area still recall this otherwise forgotten period.

From the higher slopes above Quarry Wood (27) (TQ 596441) you can see, spread out to the north, the town of Tonbridge (28) (TQ 588466), once an important prehistoric fort guarding the Medway crossing. Given by William the Conqueror to Richard Fitz-Gilbert, it became an important stronghold in Norman England.

Somerhill
Somerhill Park (32) (TQ 604451) is all that now remains from the South Frith estates attached to the domain of Tonbridge. In 1601 the Earl of Essex was executed on Tower Hill for complicity in a plot against Queen Elizabeth. Two years later, Elizabeth gave his wife, Frances, daughter of her much-loved minister, Sir Francis Walsingham, the manor of South Frith as compensation.

Since then most of this once-vast estate has been sold off, for the development of Royal Tunbridge Wells and in other numerous small parcels.

The parkland, studded with mature trees, is now an important wildlife area. The sheep-grazed area of grassland is relatively poor in terms of the flora it supports but, in season, you will find bluebells and wood anemones under the trees, and, in the damper hollows, rushes and sedges. In the marshy ground beside the stream at the western end of the site are meadow sweet and ragged robin. Woodpeckers, nuthatch, warblers and tree-creepers can be found here.

The High Weald Walk crosses a stream near Brokes Mill Farm

In Kent, Somerhill House (33) (TQ 608452) is second only to Knole in size. Frances Walsingham built this imposing mansion with the Earl of Clanrickard, her third husband. The outside is very much as it was in Jacobean times, in local sandstone, with straight-sided gables and tall brick chimney stacks.

The estate was sequestered by the Parliamentarians during the Civil Wars. After the family regained it, the heiress, Lady Musquerry, found the position ideal both to entertain her friends and for visiting the Wells when the court moved there. On one occasion her love of pleasure overcame her prudence. In her desire to provide an heir, she stuffed cushions under her skirts, claiming she carried twins. She then danced rather too energetically for her condition. The cushions fell to the ground, amid great mirth.

After various changes, Somerhill was bought by Sir Isaac Lyon Goldsmid in 1849. Sold again in 1981, there are now three schools on the site.

Many of the buildings you see around the estate were built by the Goldsmid family in the 1880s. The clock tower at the northern end, with louvred bellcote, spire and weathervane, overlooks a courtyard with extra rooms built by Sir Julian in 1879 to accommodate his eight daughters.

Park Farm (35) (TQ 615450) is in many ways a traditional Wealden farm. To the south of the path there are orchards, and on the lower slopes you will find one of the few areas in this part of the Weald where hops are still grown. Elsewhere cereals too are grown.

On the slope to the south you can see the numerous chimney shafts, the gabled roofs and moulded bargeboards of Park Farmhouse. This was built in 1850, as part of the Somerhill Home Farm. The design, also seen in the other farm buildings in the complex, recalled traditional country architecture of the previous century.

The Lodge at the entrance to Somerhill Park, built in the 1880s, in Tudor style

Tudeley
The Church of All Saints, Tudeley (36) (TQ 621454), is well worth a detour. The valley was once considered wild and remote, but the church has always thrived. The present church was rebuilt in the 18th century, with brick on an older, sandstone base. Some other parts of the earlier church survive, such as the fine chancel rails, from 1682, a small brass of a civilian and his wife (1457) and a Renaissance-style monument to George Fane (d.1572), an important local landowner, and his wife, Joan Waller.

Outstanding from this century is the stained glass window by Mark Chagall (1887-1985). This was commissioned by Sir Henry and Lady d'Avigdor Goldsmid in memory of their daughter, Sarah, who was drowned 1963. The window shows a young Christ welcoming the girl from the sea. During the 1970s and 1980s the church was further restored with 11 other commemorative windows, all by Chagall, his only work in stained glass in England.

Tudeley Woods (38 & 39) (TQ 619445 and TQ 616440), managed by the Royal Society for the Protection of Birds (RSPB) are rich in wild flowers, especially in spring. The lesser spotted woodpecker searches out invertebrates in the old wood and you may hear nightingales in mid-summer. On the higher acid Tunbridge Wells Sand to the south, standard oaks rise above coppiced ash, alder, hazel and other native trees.

The RSPB is working to restore the coppice woodland habitat which originally developed here during and after the middle ages. It has reintroduced the practice of charcoal-burning and is selling lumpwood charcoal to the barbecue market. The profits help the upkeep, while the practice enhances the wildlife species which thrive in coppiced woodland.

As you climb Knowles Bank from the north (TQ 622441) you have good views of the Greensand ridge (TQ 630550) with the North Downs (TQ 650630) beyond. You can also see the Medway gap, where the River Medway cuts its channel between both ranges.

Old Pembury

In the hollow below Church Wood (40) (TQ 625433) lies the sandstone Church of St Peter, Pembury (43) (TQ 652430). The earliest part is Norman. Coats of arms on the chancel buttresses include those of John Colepeper who gave money for the next stage, the chancel, in the 14th century. His father had forfeited the family home at Bayhall (TQ 624394), the manor to the south of Pembury, after refusing Eleanor of Aquitaine, wife of Edward I, entry to Leeds Castle. The chancel was given as a thank-offering when he regained the house.

On the right hand side of the main door is the tomb of Anne West, the last owner of Bayhall. Afraid of being buried alive, she asked that her tomb remain open. Her bailiff took food and water for a year. The tomb was only closed in 1943.

The lych-gate is a memorial to Sir Samuel Morton Peto and his wife. A prominent non-conformist and an MP, he saw a bill through parliament which allowed a non-conformist parson to conduct a burial in an Anglican churchyard. He may have been the first to be so buried himself.

The land beside you to the west of the road has been traditional grazing pasture at least since 1801. The oak and beech trees were planted as part of the parkland of Pembury Hall (TQ 624429), the vicarage until 1892. Pepper saxifrage and pignut are among the species occurring in the area of grassland. In the woodbank at the side you will find bitter vetch growing over the many mosses and lichens.

Pembury Walks (TQ 621424), once part of Pembury Woods, lost most of the spreading oaks described by Hasted in 1798 and is now largely planted with Scots pine and sweet chestnut coppice.

Somerhill, the second largest private house in Kent, now a school

The reservoir first supplied water to the area in 1885

INTERESTING FEATURES

22 Old Forge, Southborough
The forge once stood on the site of adjacent Brokes Mill Farm. There iron was worked which had been smelted at Vauxhall Furnace.

23 Viaduct
The red-brick viaduct was built in 1845 for the Tonbridge to Tunbridge Wells Railway. It has 26 arches, of varying height, according to the level of the ground.

24 Old Forge Farm
In Tudor times Old Forge farm was the site of cottages built for iron workers at the nearby forge.

25 Pond Bay
This marks the site of the Tudor water-powered Vauxhall blast furnace.

26 Forest Farm
The oast house and cottages at the farm were built in 1857 for the Somerhill estate. Some of the surrounding 200 acres have recently been planted with trees to form a new community woodland.

27 Quarry Wood
This upper slopes of this wood provided clay which was used for brick making.

28 Tonbridge
The town became an important fort beside the Medway in prehistoric times. A Norman castle stood there from the 11th century, the motte still stands at the north-west corner. A circular shell keep, surmounted by a gatehouse, dates from the 13th century.

Tonbridge School was founded in 1533 as a 'Free Grammar School'.

Castle Hill, prominent for its TV booster mast, was occupied by Celtic people from the 2nd century. They smelted iron in a bloomery on the western slopes below the fort.

29 Bournemill Farm
The farm was once a furnace, worked by the iron master John Kipping. As in many cases, hop-growing became a practical alternative once the decline of the iron industry set in.

30 A21
A road has run along the line of the A21 from London to Hastings since medieval times. It is shown on Symonson's map of 1596.

31 The Lodge
Standing at the entrance to Somerhill Park, the cottage beside the lake and the bridge were built, in Tudor style, by the Goldsmid family in the 1880s.

Link Route 1 *see page* 44

32 Somerhill Park
The park was landscaped in the 18th century. It has been identified as a site of nature conservation interest.

33 Somerhill House
The house was built by the Earl of Clanrickard and his wife, Frances Walsingham. Rainwater heads have their initials RCR and the dates 1611 and 1613.

34 Sunken path
This path beside The Toll takes the right of way from Tonbridge through to Tudeley, out of site of the inhabitants of Somerhill. The walled bridge of local sandstone linked parts of a formal garden.

35 Park Farm, oasts and farmhouse
The present buildings have been standing since the late-19th century, when hop-growing was at its height in Kent. The cowl of an oasthouse is so designed to draw the air upwards and thus create the heat required to dry the hops.

36 Church of All Saints, Tudeley
This church is one of the few in the region to be mentioned in Domesday Book. It contains some fine stained glass windows designed by Marc Chagall.

37 Crockhurst Street Farmhouse
The weatherboarded farmhouse dates from the early-17th century. The pair of cottages opposite, with red tile roofs, were built for workers on the Somerhill estate.

38 & 39 Rushpit Woods and Brakeybank Wood
These are parts of Tudeley Woods, where the remains of old bloomeries (iron works) have been found. Charcoal burning is being revived as part of a return to traditional woodland management practices.

40 Church Wood
Much of the wood, especially to the south-east, is ancient semi-natural woodland. A new planting is becoming established on the western side.

41 Kent College
An interdenominational school, Kent College was founded in Folkestone in 1886 by the Kent Wesleyan Methodist Schools Association. It moved to Hawkwell Place in 1939, on the site of the former Spring Grove house designed by Decimus Burton.

42 Hawkwell Farm
The farm recalls the name of one of the two ancient manors in this parish, officially known as Pepenbury Magna. By 1871 Hawkwell Manor had been split into three farms and had changed hands several times.

43 St Peter's Church
The old church of Pembury was first built in Norman times. Clay tiles in the roof of the nave and chancel are hand-made. Inside is a fine tie beam and kingpost roof.

St Peter's Church - Old Pembury
Early Summer

Hops growing at Park Farm, near Somerhill

3 Old Pembury - Little Bayhall

$4^1/_4$ miles - allow $2^1/_4$ hours

The High Weald Walk now takes you from old to new Pembury. On the way you pass nearby several hamlets and settlements, all flourishing communities at different times.

Fruit Farms

Downingbury (46) (TQ 630423) and Pippins (49) (TQ 637423) have been established comparitively recently as fruit farms. Until the 1950s the entire area was covered by hop gardens. As the demand for hops began to fall farmers recognised that, in spite of the steep slopes and numerous springs, the Tunbridge Wells Sand was well suited to grow fruit. At both Downingbury and Pippins you will see low-growing trees on dwarfing root stock. These make spraying and picking easier and help the critical quality control required for modern marketing. Please keep dogs on leads when passing through the fruit growing areas.

On the eastern slopes below Hepsbrook Wood (47) (TQ 633427), to the south of the A228, you will notice further changes in the area. A small vineyard, part of the Pippins estate, was planted in 1984 with French and German grapes and has produced wine since 1992.

Snipe Wood

You enter Snipe Wood (TQ 641419) from Pippins over an old brick causeway. This was the site of Keyes Mill, a water mill, which stood here until 1939. William Turner painted several water colours of it between 1795 and 1796 which are kept in London galleries. The causeway formed the dam between the upper and lower mill ponds. In the deep ghyll, ferns and other 'Atlantic' species now flourish.

Several streams drain this area. All meet in Tudeley Brook before continuing on to the Medway. Over half the trees in the wood were damaged in the 1987 storm, and many have now been cleared and replaced.

'Woodlands', on the south side of Snipe Wood

You will see large blocks of broadleaved trees, and smaller, more intimately mixed groups of broadleaves and conifers.

Romford (52) (TQ 635411) is one of the older communities of the area, isolated in its own small valley, but on the direct route from Bayham Abbey (64) (TQ 651377) to old Pembury. Until the Reformation, a priory stood on the site of the present, 19th-century house. The Abbot lived where Stanton House now stands.

Much later, an almshouse for elderly men was established here. It seems life was not easy for the inmates. Their work included breaking stones to repair the road. When the men were sick they received raisin wine, from the King William Public House on the Hastings Road. Even then they had to pay.

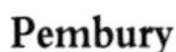

Pembury

Bo-Peep Corner (55) (TQ 634405) takes its name from a root form of Pembury. In early times, the people of Pembury were known as the Pepingas, 'look-out' people, from their position on this high ridge. The phrase 'Bon Pepin', which leads to 'Bo-Peep' is also connected. The area is shown on an 18th-century map, as Pastep Green.

The ridge has carried traffic from London to Hastings from medieval times. Pembury provided a good coaching stop on what was at one time a three-day journey to the coast. In the early days of Tunbridge Wells, the road was for a while the main route to the new spa and became still more popular. In 1709 it became the first road in Kent to be turnpiked under the new Turnpike Act. As traffic grew, people moved from old Pembury to the Upper Green where there was scope for saddlers, smiths and other workers. The shift in population was marked by the building of the new St Peter's Church (57) (TQ 626407), on land given by the Marquess Camden of Bayham in 1847. In its time, the church has seen many changes. A 92-foot spire, erected in 1886 and well-known for miles around, was removed as unsafe a hundred years later. Inside, pews have recently been removed and numerous other alterations made in order to welcome the community more openly. Repainting has enhanced the chancel.

Looking south over Great Bayhall from the Old Coach Road

To the south of the by-pass (TQ 630403) you will find a broad track between old hedges which continues due south and eventually drops steeply to a clearing. Now a green lane, this track was once a coach road (60) (TQ 629403) from Bayham Abbey (64) (TQ 651377) to Pembury. A picnic site (61) (TQ 629397) marks a junction on the old coach road from where another track led up to Pastep Green. The deep pool here, resulting from one of the numerous springs on the hillside, provided a good watering place before the last climb to the Pembury ridge.

Bayhall

The cluster of farm buildings below you is all that remains of Bayhall (62) (TQ 624394), the old manor house of

Pepenbury Parva, the southern of the two manors of Pembury. This was the home of John Colepeper who added the chancel to the old church at Pembury in the 14th century. His family had owned the site since the 12th century and remained there for around 400 years. In the 16th century a number of well-connected families owned Bayhall in rapid succession, but none stayed long. Robert Sackville, Earl of Dorset, who bought the house in 1610 was one of these. Perhaps the low-lying position contributed to this. The slopes behind Bayhall were at this time heavily wooded, and roads throughout the area were extremely poor.

The Amherst family, whose memorials are in the old church, then settled here and built a new house, shown in paintings with Jacobean chimneys, mansard roofs and dormer windows.

The High Weald Walk near Great Bayhall

The last person of means to live at Bayhall was Anne West, whose tomb lay open beside the door in the parish church. After her death, the estate was acquired by the Earl, later the Marquess, Camden of Bayham in 1799. The house then fell into ruins. Anne West inevitably returned to haunt the site and Bayhall was demolished early in the 20th century.

Until the end of the last century, land to either side of the lane south of Little Bayhall (63) (TQ 618394) was heavily wooded. Another small woodland, Oakes Wood, covered the small spur below Little Bayhall Farmhouse.

INTERESTING FEATURES

44 Reservoir
Naturally formed from a widening in the Alder stream, the reservoir was used from 1885 to provide the water for the region.

45 House
The house on the corner of Church Road and Redwings Lane was built as the manager's dwelling in 1890.

46 Downingbury
The farmhouse dates from the early-18th century, its farm buildings now converted into separate dwellings. The weatherboarded barn dates from the 17th century.

47 Vineyard
A vineyard, planted in 1984, brings further variety to an area where traditional hop growing has already yielded to new orchards.

48 Orchards
Careful research has produced top fruit which meets exacting demands. Apples, pears, plums and cherries are all sold on the national market.

The farm shop at Downingbury is open seven days a week throughout the year. You can also pause at Pippins farm shop for teas and refreshments in the fruit season.

49 Pippins
The oast, built in 1830 and now disused, is another reminder of the hop gardens which covered this area until the 1950s.

50 Stone Court Farm
Keyes Mill, a water mill, stood near the farm until 1939. William Turner painted several water-colours of it

Farming continues to shape the character of the High Weald landscape

between 1795 and 1796 which may be found in London galleries.

51 Lower Green, Pembury
This area formed the centre of a thriving community based on the Stone Court Brick and Tile Company. This was well-known for its hard paving blocks used at one time throughout south-east England.

52 Romford
A priory stood on the site of the present house until the Reformation. It was dissolved by Cardinal Wolsey, along with many others.

53 Stantons
The Abbot's House stood on the site of the present Stantons. Later, an almshouse provided home and work for old men.

54 Mays Barn
Mays Barn, weatherboarded and underbuilt with red brick, dates from the 16th century. Its style is typical of many barns in the High Weald.

55 Bo-Peep Corner
The sign of the shepherdess recalls the old name, connected with Bon Pepin, from which Pembury may be derived. It marks the site of another small community once known as Pastep Green.

56 'King William'
This public house is easily recognisable by its sign near the High Weald Walk. A public house has stood on this site since 1799.

57 St Peter's Church
Built in 1847 and set back from the road, the sandstone tower of St. Peter's Church is easily seen from the open countryside around.

58 Upper Green
The Upper Green became the new centre for Pembury in the 19th century with the coming of the stage coach. Traffic on the London to Hastings road brought a considerable increase in business.

Water trough
Standing on the Green, the water trough is dedicated to the memory of Margery Polley. She was burnt at the stake at Tonbridge in 1555 for refusing to accept Roman Catholicism.

'Camden Arms'
This timber-framed building hung with peg-tiles was formerly known as the Camden Hotel. It was famous for its garden and tennis courts. The sign is taken from quarterings on the Camden Coat of Arms, charged with the three elephants which became a familiar sign throughout the Bayham estates.

Almshouses

Built in 1715, the almshouses were given by Charles Amherst who lived at Bayhall. They were maintained by the Camden estate from 1799 until 1953, then handed over to the Charity Commissioners.

59 Woodsgate

The Woodsgate Coaching Inn provided an important stopping place for travellers on the London to Hastings Road. In 1785 the landlady welcomed up to 14 coaches a day.

60 Coach Road

Now a green lane, the road ran here from Bayham Abbey to Pembury. The White Canons used it when they visited the old church of St Peter's, whose patronage they held.

61 Picnic site

This area marks a junction on the old coach road from where another track led up to Pastep Green. The woods here continued without a break to Chalket Woods.

62 Bayhall

This was once the old manor house of Pepenbury Parva, the southern of the two manors of Pepenbury. A Jacobean house stood here until the early-20th century on the site of an earlier 12th-century building.

63 Little Bayhall

Little Bayhall was surrounded by thick woodland until the last century. The land was cleared to provide grazing for sheep.

Beehives and Orchards at Pippins - Early summer

64 Bayham Abbey
Long in ruins, Bayham Abbey stood six miles away beside the River Teise west of Lamberhurst. Its brethren, known as White Canons, belonged to an order who followed the version of the Augustinian rule established at Premontre in France and introduced to England in 1140. They had considerable influence on the surrounding countryside both as landowners and religious supervisors. They were among the first to be dissolved by Cardinal Wolsey to fund his new colleges at Ipswich and Oxford.

4 Little Bayhall - Chase Wood

$3^1/_4$ miles - allow $1^3/_4$ hours

Bluebells in abundance near Ely Grange

Ridgeway

High Woods Lane (65) (TQ 614390) follows the line of an old ridgeway which ran from the Upper Green at Pembury past Chalket Woods (TQ 623403) and on down the steep slope beside Palmers Farm (67) (TQ 609383). The farmers from Bayhall used it regularly as they took their corn to be ground at Benhall Mill (71) (TQ 608376).

At its highest point the ridge rises to 136 metres and gives clear views towards Cranbrook. The valleys below collect water from the numerous springs which occur at the junction of the sandstone and clay. The streams so formed join others to form the Teise at Dundale Farm (TQ 631384), whose triple oasts you can see beside it.

Looking south-west from High Wood, near Hawkenbury

High Wood

Mature oaks in High Wood (66) (TQ 605427) have survived, despite the force of the 1987 storm. Although there were casualties, much has now been replanted. As well as sweet chestnut coppice, some hazel, hornbeam, birch, goat willow and ash remain from the ancient woodland. In spring you will find carpets of bluebells and anemones.

Hawkenbury

To the south of High Wood, the route skirts Hawkenbury (TQ 596387). This remained a small hamlet until late into the 19th century. It was long known as Tutty's Village, after one James Tutty of Brenchley who, like Marjorie Polley at Pembury, was martyred in the reign of Queen Mary.

In the 19th century Tutty's Village consisted largely of farm labourers, railway workers and brickmakers from the two brick works in the area. It acquired a reputation for unruliness until philanthropists stepped in and organised a Sunday School for the children.

Whatever was thought about the inhabitants, the land was considered valuable as farmland. In 1853 the land became part of the Camden estate at a cost of £2,500. You can see a medallion bearing the Camden elephant on one of a pair of farmworkers cottages. These cottages are the only buildings which survive from the 19th century, along with the 'Spread Eagle' (TQ 596385) on the corner of Forest Road, Hawkenbury Farmhouse (TQ

602383) which stands beside the corner of the High Weald route and Tutty's Farm (TQ 602381) itself.

Hawkenbury was originally part of Frant parish. At the end of the 19th century it was considered too remote, its people more a part of Tunbridge Wells, and a drawback to the smooth administration of Frant parish. In 1894 it was included in Kent. Reynards Brook (69) (TQ 601379), one of the tributaries of the River Teise, now marks the boundary between Kent and Sussex.

Farmsteads

The slopes beside Windmill Farm (71) (TQ 599905) on either side of Reynards Brook are set-aside from traditional farmland. Now the land forms an important wildlife haven between built-up areas. A series of springs maintain moist, boggy ground, especially on the central slopes. You may find marsh violet, bog asphodel and bog pimpernel as well as mosses and sedges. At the northern edge of this area you will see the remains of an old nut orchard. The hedgerows and shaws contain oak, holly and alder.

The area marks the old boundaries between the great Camden and Abergavenny estates. The Nevill Golf Course (72) (TQ 595374), bearing the Abergavenny family name, covers 200 acres of land where the Nevills once raced and exercised horses. The Golf Club was founded in 1914 and now measures 6,336 yards. It was redesigned after the War by Mr Henry Cotton. Contemporary golfing members include Paul Way and Jamie Spence.

The number of farms clustered on the slopes below the Bayham Road are witness both to the many springs which appear here and to the old drovers' track in the valley. You follow one of these in the short stretch of Tangier Lane (75) (TQ 592368) taken by the High Weald Walk beside Brickhouse Farm (74) (TQ 593368).

In the 17th century this was a busy route, running past Tangier Farm (76) (TQ 588368) and Brook Farm (77) (TQ 594368), to link with roads to Kippings Cross (TQ 646390) and

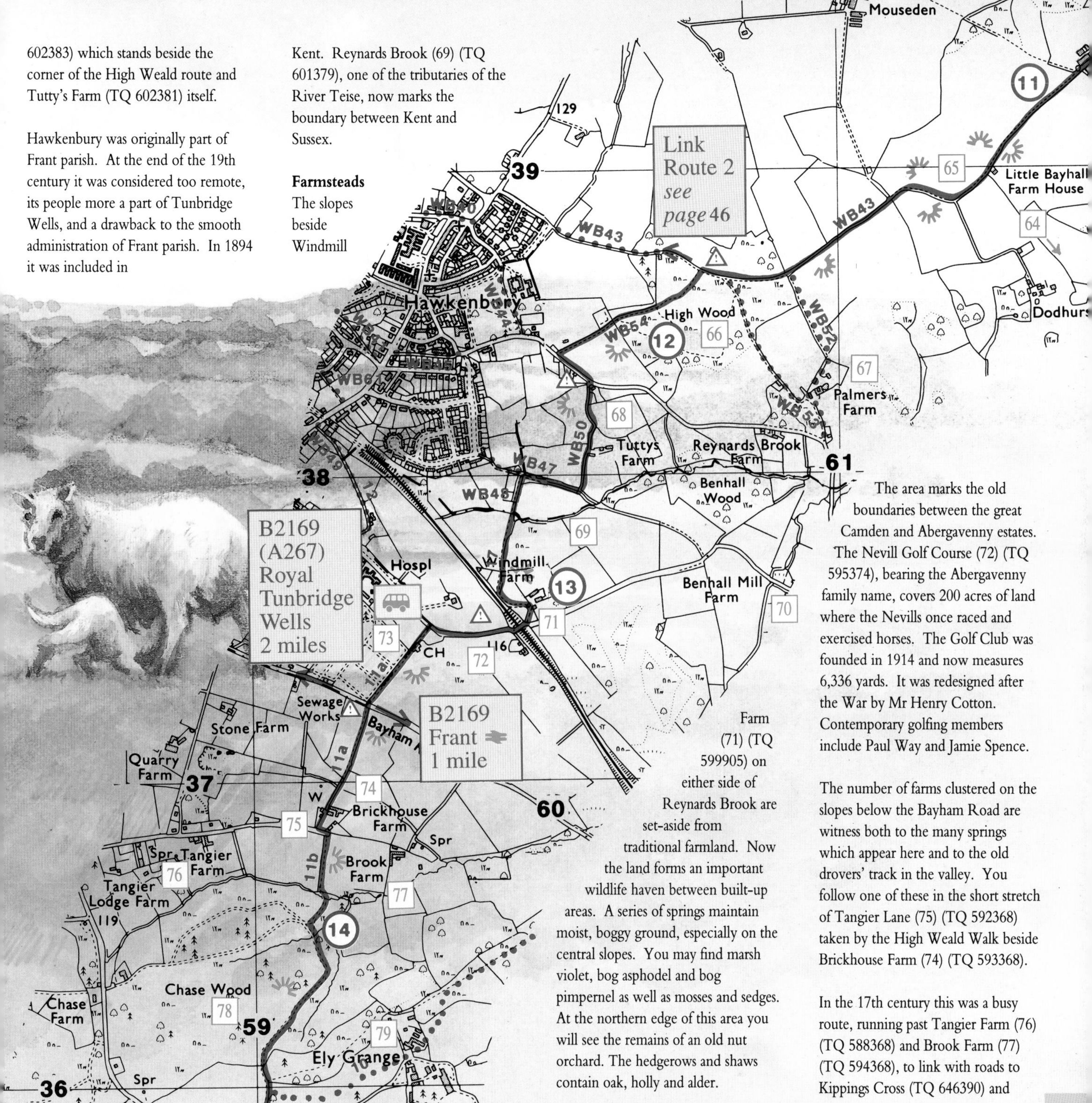

Chase Wood has been partly replanted since the 1987 storm

Bayham Abbey (TQ 651377). In the 18th century, as Tunbridge Wells increased in popularity, traffic favoured the Bayham Road, along the slightly higher, drier ground.

Brickhouse Farm and granary, built in local brick, stand on land once known as Fitness Farm. The ornate 'A' above each of two windows of the farmhouse shows you are on land once belonging to the Earl of Abergavenny. The chimneys, double gable roof and the yellow brick round windows and corners are typical of estate buildings of their time. The first-floor granary built over other sheds reveals a time of plenty in cereal production.

At Brook Farm, across the field, you see the standard, multi-purpose barn, with low roof and hipped end.

The northern boundary of Chase Wood (78) (TQ 597363) runs along the bottom of a deep-cut ghyll where the Wadhurst Clay has been gouged out to form one of the many tributaries of the Teise. On the slopes you will see Scots pine, oak and larch replanted after the 1987 storm, as well as sweet chestnut coppice, a mixture of other broadleaved trees and conifers.

Sixteenth-century records show Ely Grange (79) (TQ 595361) as Helly Grange. The name relates to the initial process in iron working, when the ore, newly-extracted nearby, was washed, then burned (elyed) before being taken to the furnace. Various houses have stood on this site. The present house, in neo-Georgian style, was built in 1932. The cedars were planted in the last century.

INTERESTING FEATURES

65 High Woods Lane
This lane follows the line of an old ridgeway which ran from the Upper Green at Pembury to Benhall Mill.

66 High Wood
The wood still contains remnants of ancient woodland. Its lower slopes are carpeted with bluebells in spring.

67 Palmers Farm
Traces remain of the old ridgeway, seen in the brick bonds which survive in the footpath. Hops grew here at the turn of the century.

68 Tutty's Farm
The farm recalls an old name for Hawkenbury, Tutty's Village, named after James Tutty from Brenchley. Brickworks stood to its west and on the field now used as the recreation ground.

69 Reynards Brook
One of the tributaries of the River Teise, Reynards Brook now marks the boundary between Kent and Sussex.

70 Benhall Mill
The mill was a flourishing forge in the days of the iron industry, often under the same ownership as Dundale Forge. It later became a corn mill.

71 Windmill Farm
The land surrounding Windmill Farm has become an important wildlife haven between built-up areas. An old nut-orchard lies in the north-west corner.

72 Nevill Golf Course
Covering 200 acres of land which the Nevills of Eridge Park once used as a 'horse course', the 18-hole golf course was founded in 1914.

73 Tunbridge Wells Borough Cemetery
The cemetery first opened in 1874.

74 Brickhouse Farm
Brickhouse Farm was built as part of the Abergavenny estate to high standards. An ornate 'A' is clearly visible marking the original ownership.

75 Tangier Lane
Once called Ivylodge Lane, Tangier Lane is an old drovers' road, which led to Benhall Mill, then on towards Bayham Abbey.

76 Tangier Farm
The farm belonged to an ex-soldier who bought the land from savings acquired when he had served in the garrison at Tangiers. The Portuguese Catherine de Braganza bought Tangier as part of her dowry when she married Charles II in 1660.

77 Brook Farm
Brook Farm stands on the site of an earlier farm known as Ivylodge Farm. It was connected with Ivylodge, the oldest house in the area, half a mile to the north-west.

78 Chase Wood
Replanted after the 1987 storm with Scots pine, oak and larch. The deep-cut ghyll at the bottom forms a tributary of the River Teise.

79 Ely Grange
Dating from the 16th century, Ely Grange was once known as Helly Grange. The present house, in neo-Georgian style, with coach house, stables and clock tower, was built in 1932.

Brickhouse Farm was built for the Abergavenny Estate

5 Chase Wood - Eridge Green

$3^1/_4$ miles - allow $1^3/_4$ hours

Frant

The village of Frant (TQ 590354), (the fern-covered heath) was cleared and settled from Saxon times. At an altitude of 166 metres and with grazing for herds and a natural dew pond on the common, it was a safe and useful, if remote, settlement in the middle of the Waterdown Forest. At first Frant formed part of the Rotherfield Parish. A small chapel was established in 1103, and it became independent by the end of that century.

The George Inn, on Frant High Street, dates from 1742

In the late middle ages, villagers earned their living from the iron works in the valleys. As the iron industry declined they returned to agriculture, selling goods in the now developing Tunbridge Wells. The neat village is now much changed from days when it took six oxen to pull one lady through the mud to the church.

The present Church of St Alban's (80) (TQ 590356) was redesigned and completed by 1821. Inside you will find an unusually short and wide nave. The slender columns, in the Victorian Perpendicular style, are made of iron, with leaf moulding on the capitals picked out in gold on red. Iron is also used for the columns supporting the gallery and for the tracery of the windows. You will see the arms of the two neighbouring landowners on either side of the chancel steps. On the north side you find the red rose on grey saltire of the Nevill's, on the south side, the elephants and stars of the Camden household.

In the churchyard, family tragedies figure clearly. One couple, John and Mary Diggins, buried under yews on the east side, lost one son, William, aged 27, from wounds received in the Crimean War, another, John, in 1858 aged 34, in one of the accidents frequent in the early days of rail. They also lost a daughter Elizabeth, aged 16, and another son, Thomas, aged 27, but themselves lived to old age.

The memorial, beside the west path, remembers Lieutenant Colonel John By of the Royal Engineers of Shernfold Park (84) (TQ 590351), who lived from 1783 to 1836. Within the church is another memorial to him, on the south wall.

John By was chosen, in 1826, to organise a canal scheme to enable ships up to 110 feet long to proceed up the Ottawa River, to Kingston, Lake Ontario. This entailed building 42 locks. Colonel By arranged accommodation for the many labourers. The carefully planned site, originally called Bytown, was renamed Ottawa by Queen Victoria. The Canadian parliament stands on the site of the former barracks.

As you look west from Frant, you see the broad slopes of the Weald stretching as far as Ashdown Forest (TQ 460310). The land immediately to the north and south once formed the 6,000-acre Waterdown Forest, part of the extensive parish of Rotherfield six miles to the south. After Norman times, it remained for several generations in the possession of the Clares of Tonbridge, to many just an extension of the South Frith forest adjoining it to the North. A royal hunting area like the Ashdown Forest, it maintained its woodland cover until Tudor Times.

Eridge Park

Eridge Park (TQ 570110), the largest and oldest deer park in England, still covers 2,500 acres of this land. It has been held by the Earls and Marquesses of Abergavenny for over 500 years. Their ancestor, Hugh le Despencer, received it from Edward III in 1338. The Nevills, a Norman family who first settled in Lincolnshire and later in Westmorland, acquired Eridge Park when Edward Nevill, the youngest son of the first Earl of Westmorland, and grandson of John of Gaunt, married the heiress to the estate, nine year old Elizabeth. The family has figured in national affairs on many important occasions.

Eridge Park contains a wealth of wildlife. In the woods, all three British woodpeckers may be heard, and you will see oaks several centuries old. As you pass over the bay (87) (TQ 571349) between the two eastern lakes, once pen ponds for the nearby forge and furnace, you will see the emerald of dragonflies, and the browns and reds of butterflies. A glance along the water will show much aquatic life.

On the slopes of Eridge Old Park (85) (TQ 580344) to the south, bloomeries

19th-century gravestones, memorials to the Diggins family, at St Alban's Church, Frant

have been found, where Celts and Romans from the ancient hill fort of Saxonbury (86) (TQ 578330) smelted iron. More recently, in the 18th century, smugglers used old caves nearby to hide their loot when chased by the militia. A folly built in the 19th century stands on the summit.

Like most landowners of the time, the Abergavennys utilised the iron found on their slopes to the full. Eridge Furnace (90) (TQ 564340) and Eridge Forge (91) (TQ 560350) flourished under the name in the late-16th century. The lakes, now landscaped, give little evidence of their industrial past but you can still find forge cinder in the bed of the stream by the most westerly bay (TQ 559351), and signs of the wheel pit beside the footbridge.

With all the resources of the Waterdown Forest, it must have been easy at first to find fuel for the iron industry. But here, as elsewhere, the woods were ravaged by iron-workers' demands for charcoal. An Act of Parliament in 1585 tried to redress the balance by forbidding new iron works. At Eridge, local people found their own solution. Tenants on the Abergavenny land who held old rights to allow their pigs to forage in the forest, refused to pay their dues. They won a case in the early-17th century, presumably with simple logic - no trees, no acorns, no pigs. Specimen trees planted in the 19th century

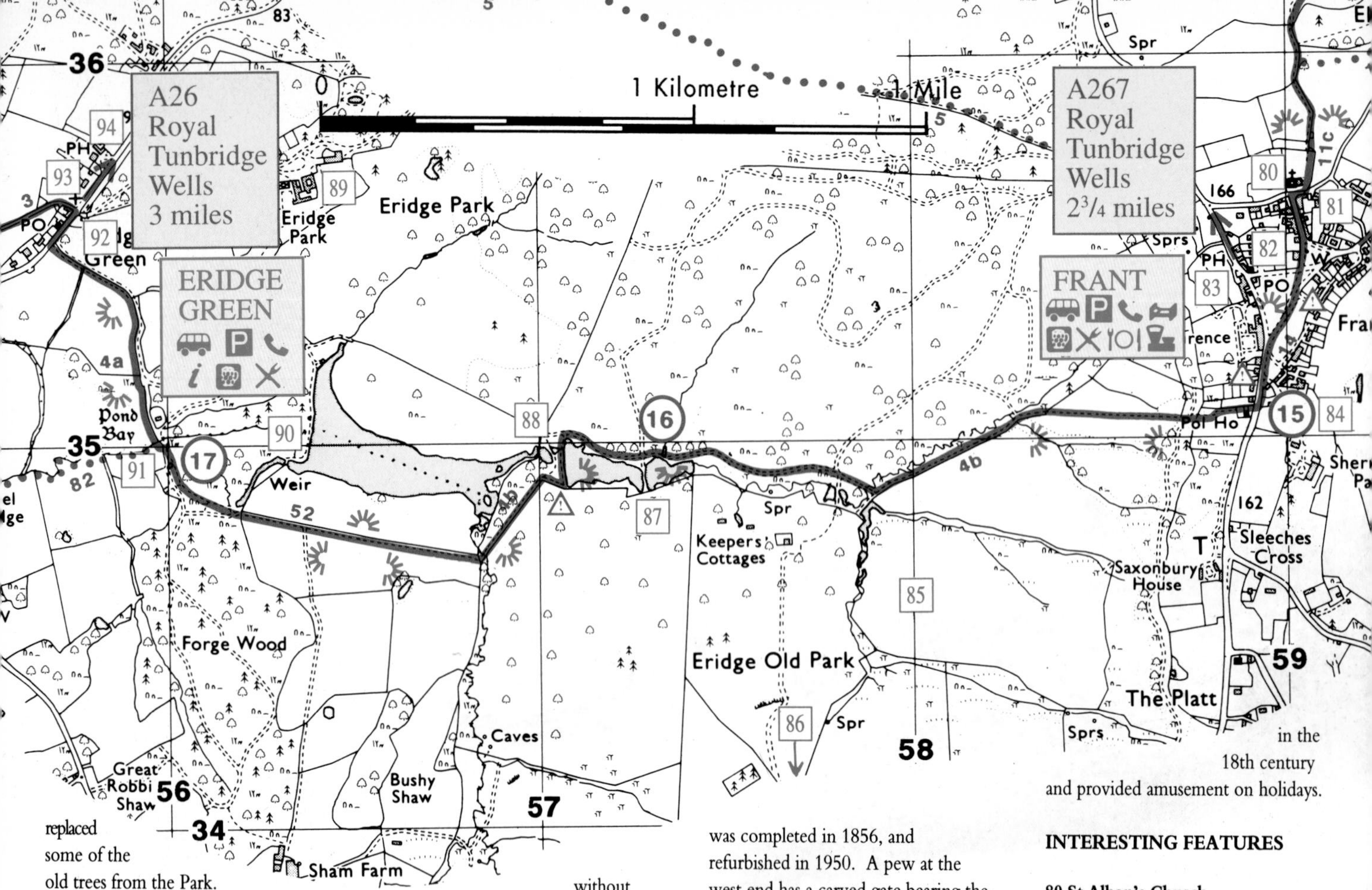

replaced some of the old trees from the Park.

A mansion has long stood at Eridge Castle (89) (TQ 563356). Queen Elizabeth rested there for six days when she travelled through Kent and Sussex in the summer of 1573, receiving the French ambassador during her stay. Her journey was considered not without risks, the countryside wild and dangerous, worse than anything she had encountered in the Peak District. The first building was replaced by a castle, designed in Gothic style, in 1789. Always mocked for its extravagant style, it was replaced by a new house in 1938.

Autumn in Eridge Park

Eridge Green

Eridge Green, originally a small clearing in the forest, grew up as a collection of houses built for the Eridge estate workers in the 19th century.

The former parish at Eridge Green was first created by amalgamating parts of Frant and Rotherfield. The Church of The Holy Trinity (93) (TQ 557357) was completed in 1856, and refurbished in 1950. A pew at the west end has a carved gate bearing the Abergavennys' heraldic device and motto - ne vile velis ('desire nothing common'). The woodcarving, many of them with roses or woodland flowers, are the work of George Swaysland, master carver, of Burgess Hill. The eagle on the lectern was carved by a Pole, J Rioko.

The 'Nevill Crest and Gun' (94) (TQ 558357) added the Abergavenny family name in 1860. Before that it was known simply as 'The Gun'. In addition to iron works, the Abergavennys owned two gunneries to enable the local people to practice shooting. Cast at Eridge Furnace, one of the guns still stood outside the inn in the 18th century and provided amusement on holidays.

INTERESTING FEATURES

80 St Alban's Church

Rebuilt in 1821, the battlements on the tower enclosed the old spire to save the extra cost of rebuilding it. The modern lych-gate has a hexagonal cover. It was erected in memory of those who

taught at The Limes School 1851-1888, and at Hazelhirst School 1888-1940.

81 George Inn

Built in 1742 on the site of a 16th-century cottage, the 'George' served a travelling public when the High Street was the main through route.

Frant 1 1/3 miles

Three-bay house
Situated on the east side of the road with angle buttress-shafts and battlements, this house recalls the Gothic style favoured by Lord Abergavenny in the 18th century.

Wells
The well at the southern end of the High Street is the Victoria Memorial Well (TQ 591355). Its twin, the Albert Memorial Well (TQ 587356), lies on the A267 overlooking Eridge Park.

82 Frant School
The School with its double fronted gables, was founded in 1816.

83 'Abergavenny Arms'
This public house on the A267 dates from about 1480 when it stood in a small clearing in woodland. It was once called 'The Bull' after the crest and supporters on the Nevill arms.

84 Shernfold Park
A farm dating from the 13th century. The present house, once home of Lieutenant Colonel John By, founder of Ottawa, was built in early Victorian times.

85 Eridge Old Park
Once part of the Royal Chase of Waterdown Forest, Eridge Park is the largest and oldest deer park in England. Celtic and Roman bloomeries have been found on the southern slopes as well as caves, used by smugglers in the 18th century.

86 Saxonbury Hill
A hill fort stood on Saxonbury Hill. Iron Age Celts settled before and during the Roman occupation. A 19th-century folly now stands on top of the hill.

87 Bay
The dam between the two eastern parts of the lake served to maintain pen ponds for the iron works to the west.

88 Eridge Park
The landscaped gardens south of Eridge Castle contain many trees planted by visiting dignitaries in Victorian times.

89 Eridge Castle
Eridge Castle was built in 1787 on the site of a former house where Elizabeth I had stayed. It was demolished to make way for the present house in 1938.

90 Eridge Furnace
In Tudor times, the furnace lay at the western end of the lake. Now landscaped, the area shows little sign of the once intense industrial activity.

91 Eridge Forge
There are still traces of forge cinder in the stream. Signs of the wheel pit have also been found beside the Pond Bay.

92 Staircase Cottage
The cottage was built as the schoolhouse in 1860. It took in between 60 and 70 children.

The village sign at Eridge Green

93 Holy Trinity Church
The church was completed in 1856 for the growing community beside the Park. The parish was first formed by amalgamating parts of Frant and Rotherfield.

94 'Nevill Crest and Gun'
This public house has a gun standing nearby which provided gunnery practice until the 18th century.

Eridge Park and lake — Autumn.

6 Eridge Green - Old Groombridge

$4^1/_4$ miles - allow $2^1/_4$ hours

Eridge Green (TQ 557356) - 'the eagles ridge' - was once wild and remote. Now some plantations of both broadleaves and conifers stretch to the north-east but, on the higher ground especially, the woodland has changed little since the middle ages when the Waterdown Forest was a royal hunting ground, and The Warren (TQ 555364) to the north was reserved for hare and rabbit.

Eridge Rocks

At Eridge Rocks (95) (TQ 554358) you will find some of the outcrops which gave the place its aura of romance and wilderness. Here the Ardingly sandstone forms cliffs over 30 feet high. You will see a number of empty fissures where the vertical joints have opened out, through weathering by frost. The dark appearance arises where iron oxides have been redeposited.

The sandstone rests on impervious clay and so retains moisture. The woodland cover helps to create a warm micro-climate where species from the warm 'Atlantic' period flourish such as the Tunbridge filmy fern. You will also find liverworts and mosses, as well as swathes of bluebells and dog's mercury in season.

The large acreage at Warren Farm (97) (TQ 552358), unusual in the High Weald, marks a tendency of recent years to amalgamate fields to facilitate production and cut costs. At the western end you will find a narrow shaw lying in the hollow which links two blocks of ancient woodland, The Warren and Birchett's Wood.

Harrison's Rocks have provided a training ground for many Everest climbers

Park Corner (98) (TQ 539360) marks the edge of the Abergavenny estate. You can see Eridge Park on the skyline as you take the path beside Pinstraw Farm (99) (TQ 537357) and Birchden Wood (100) (TQ 533358). From Tudor times a series of owners took advantage of the stream to forge iron. Birchden Forge (TQ 533353) operated with Hamsell Furnace (TQ 538344), producing guns and other munitions.

Harrison's Rocks

One owner, William Harrison, made fire-arms there as late as 1750. When demand for his product finally declined he turned his land to other uses, opening it to the many visitors who now came to admire the scenery. Harrison's Rocks (102) (TQ 532357), which provided the main attraction, another outcrop of Ardingly stone, are now owned by the British Mountaineering Council. In places they reach 40 feet. They offer high grade ascents and have been a training ground for 11 Everest climbers.

Groombridge

Until the mid-19th century, Groombridge (TQ 531374) remained a small village, with very few houses south of the Grom. Then the Goldsmiths' Company, owners of the nearby Birchden estate, pressed for railway access.

The London, Brighton and South Coast Railway's branch line from Three Bridges to East Grinstead was extended to Groombridge in 1865, and to Tunbridge Wells the year after. For over 100 years Groombridge remained an important railway junction, with lines to Kent as well as Sussex and London. The triangular junction was achieved in 1914. Groombridge station (TQ 533372) was particularly busy during the 1939-45 war. In the 1950s 10 trains passed through an hour. The station was finally closed in 1985.

The arrival of the railway immediately brought new residents. Glen Andred (101) (TQ 528357), prominent on the slopes, with its dormers, gables, chimney stacks and hung tiles, was one of several country houses built by Norman Shaw to accommodate wealthier incomers. More general development continued until the 1950s.

On the slopes to the north of the Grom (TQ 531376), you see the houses of old Groombridge (111) (TQ 530377). The old village traces its history back to Saxon times when Gromenbregge, the fortification by the Grom, defended this outpost of the kingdom of Kent.

Groombridge Place

At the centre stands Groombridge Place (109) (TQ 533376), a moated manor house. It was here that, according to tradition, Richard Waller brought Charles, Duc d'Orleans, as a hostage after the Battle of Agincourt. Richard was knighted and his coat of arms bears the escutcheon of the French house of Orleans, with the motto: 'huc fructus virtutis' (Hither the results of courage!)

In 1618 John Packer bought the house. His son, Philip Packer, a clerk to the Privy Seal during the reign of Charles II and also a founder member of the Royal Society, built the present house in 1662. From the Walk you see a short, Italianate flight of steps and colonnaded porch set within the Elizabethan 'H' plan. Inside is superb Jacobean panelling. Even the Elizabethan chimneys suggest affluence, as these were taxed at £1 per year.

The diarist John Evelyn (1620-1706) was a frequent visitor. The garden on the north side today remains very much as he advised in the 1670s, with formal paths laid to lawn, yew hedges and topiary.

Birchden Junction signal box controlled the divergence of the lines to Oxted and Tunbridge Wells West. Reproduced from 'Branch Lines to Tunbridge Wells' (Middleton Press)

In the last century, Groombridge Place became the property of the Reverend John Saint, rector of Speldhurst, whose daughters lived here until 1918. The Saint sisters were well-known both for their generosity, and for an interest in the supernatural. These interests combined when Miss Saint laid the ghost of an apprentice who had been ill-treated. To help him to his rest, Miss Saint brought in a coach load of apprentices and feasted them well.

Old Groombridge

The Church of St John (110) (TQ 531377) was built on the site of an older chapel in 1625 as a private chapel to Groombridge Place. It was a thank-offering for the safe return of Prince Charles from Spain, dedicated early in the year he was crowned King. You can see the panache of King James I carved over the porch door, and the Latin inscription referring to the future King.

Inside you will find six stained glass windows by Charles Kempe, with the wheatsheaf he used as his trademark. Kempe may well have taken the idea of peacock feathers included in the designs, and recurrent in all his work, from the peacocks which roamed at Groombridge Place. Throughout the series of windows, you can see the story of Groombridge, its owners and benefactors, interwoven with powerful images of Christ, the evangelists and the saints.

The past owners of Groombridge Place are recalled elsewhere in the churchyard. The tombs at the church door are those of the Camfield family, owners from 1754. The clock on the church wall recalls Robert and Sarah Burges, owners in the early-19th century.

The Crown Inn (111) (TQ 531377) and other buildings around the green (TQ 531376) at old Groombridge form a picturesque group of 16th to 18th-century village cottages, with oak frames and hung tiles, weatherboarding and peg tiles. Now private dwellings, these houses were shops at the turn of the century, with a colourful group of shop-owners who maintained the traditions of old Groombridge.

INTERESTING FEATURES

95 Eridge Rocks
These are outcrops of weathered Ardingly sandstone. Their moist micro-climate supports rare 'Atlantic' species.

96 The Warren
These slopes are covered with broadleaved and conifer plantations. Remnants of ancient woodland exist along the southern side.

Picturesque houses surround the Green at old Groombridge

97 Warren Farm
A bull's head over a barn doorway at Warren Farm can be seen from the path, a reminder that this was once Abergavenny land.

98 Park Corner
Land in this area was owned by the Goldsmiths' Company from 1856-1937. Their coat of arms, now painted over, still appears on the wall of the corner house, once The Goldsmiths' Arms.

99 Pinstraw Farm
The farm originally formed part of the manor of Birchden. It was the property of the Goldsmiths' Company during the 19th and early-20th centuries.

100 Forge Farm
The farm stands on the site of Birchden Forge. There cannon and ammunition were produced until the mid-18th century.

Groombridge Place, a 17th century moated manor house

101 Glen Andred
This house was designed by the influential Victorian architect, Norman Shaw, in 1867. The old English style was typical of much of the Arts and Crafts Movement, of which he was a member.

102 Harrison's Rocks
Harrison's Rocks are an extensive range of weathered Ardingly sandstone, much used by climbers. They provided a great attraction to early visitors.

103 Birchden Wood
The wood suffered badly in the 1987 storm but already new growth, mainly of birch and other broadleaves, has established itself. The wood can be further explored using a network of woodland trails.

104 Footbridge
This unusually broad footbridge for pedestrians, with steps for extra length, first served as a bridge for vehicles in London dockland. It was introduced here to enable villagers to cross to the spring.

105 Church of St Thomas the Apostle
This church was built to a design of Norman Shaw in local stone in 1884. The church has three stained glass windows by Charles Kempe, and a tile-hung bell turret.

106 Corseley Road
The road takes its name from a farm built for Richard Maynard who died at 'Cozleigh' in 1613.

107 Victoria Inn
This public house was built on the site of three toll cottages. A toll used to be levied at two pence per person. When the miller provided a by-pass at only one penny, the inn clearly benefited.

Mile Post
The post marks the site of the turnpike where dues were paid for the upkeep of the road. The Roman numeral IV indicates the distance from Tunbridge Wells.

Florence Farm
This farm is the oldest one in the area. It has stood here since the 16th century.

108 Road bridge
The rusticated sandstone bridge marks the county boundary. It was built towards the end of the 18th century.

Mill
Situated at Mill House, the mill was last used in 1923. It still contains some of the original workings.

109 Groombridge Place
The present house was built in the 17th century, on the site of the old moated manor house. Its first recorded owner, William Russell, and his wife, endowed the chapel to St John in 1239. The gardens are now open to the public.

110 St John's Church
Built in 1628 in red brick, St. John's Church has an unusual porch where

Const & Co
Fores
Way
52

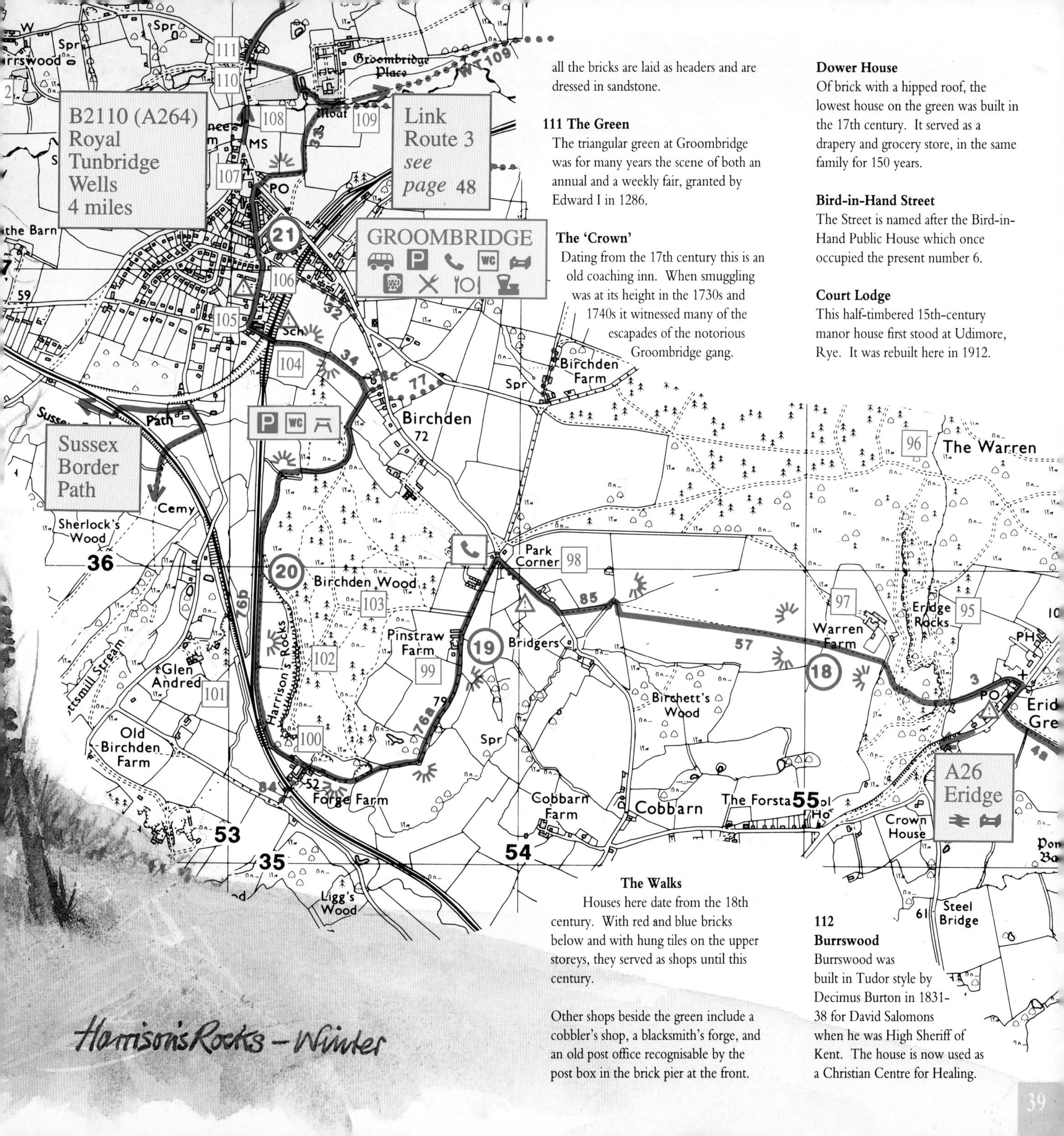

Harrison's Rocks – Winter

all the bricks are laid as headers and are dressed in sandstone.

111 The Green

The triangular green at Groombridge was for many years the scene of both an annual and a weekly fair, granted by Edward I in 1286.

The 'Crown'

Dating from the 17th century this is an old coaching inn. When smuggling was at its height in the 1730s and 1740s it witnessed many of the escapades of the notorious Groombridge gang.

The Walks

Houses here date from the 18th century. With red and blue bricks below and with hung tiles on the upper storeys, they served as shops until this century.

Other shops beside the green include a cobbler's shop, a blacksmith's forge, and an old post office recognisable by the post box in the brick pier at the front.

Dower House

Of brick with a hipped roof, the lowest house on the green was built in the 17th century. It served as a drapery and grocery store, in the same family for 150 years.

Bird-in-Hand Street

The Street is named after the Bird-in-Hand Public House which once occupied the present number 6.

Court Lodge

This half-timbered 15th-century manor house first stood at Udimore, Rye. It was rebuilt here in 1912.

112

Burrswood

Burrswood was built in Tudor style by Decimus Burton in 1831-38 for David Salomons when he was High Sheriff of Kent. The house is now used as a Christian Centre for Healing.

7 Old Groombridge - Bullingstone

$2^1/_4$ miles - allow $1^1/_2$ hours

The hill behind Groombridge rises steeply from 60 metres at the green to 125 metres at Top Hill Farm, in under half a mile. On the slopes you pass through Beech Wood (113) (TQ 531379). Beside the path you will see some sweet chestnut, but much of this wood contains remnants of ancient woodland.

The ground you tread here and to the north above Beech Wood was once part of a broad delta where sediment was deposited over millions of years, then compressed, by the weight of later deposits of clay and chalk, into sandstone. The slopes of the valley were formed at the end of the cretaceous period, when violent earth movements forced parts of the earth here upwards along fault lines. Subsequent weathering first removed the chalk from the dome, then gradually eroded the Wealden clays to reveal the sandstone beneath.

As a result, the soil changes from the rich alluvium of the valley below to the sandier soil found on the higher ground. In spite of the poorer quality of the soil, Top Hill Farm (114) (TQ 533383) has produced cereal over several centuries and sustained a fine pedigree herd of cattle.

From the highest point, at 130 metres (TQ 534384), you can enjoy fine views of Ashdown Forest (TQ 460310), Broadwater Forest (TQ 552375), Saxonbury Hill (TQ 578350) and Crowborough (TQ 518306).

Ashurst

The busy A264 (115) (TQ 535390) was once a packhorse lane which carried heavy traffic to and from the furnace and forge at Ashurst (TQ 508389) beside the Medway. Long known as Sandy Lane, furniture on its way to the ironworks in Ashurst regularly passed that way, even in winter. Iron and brass guns for the Navy and for export to Holland equally regularly trundled back to join the main road north at Gipps Cross (TQ 551392).

The imposing, white mansion to the west is Fernchase Manor. Until recently known as Ashurst Park (120) (TQ 532395), it was built between 1830 and 1840 on the site of an earlier house, with 15 bedrooms and much stabling. Owned latterly by the Right Hon. the Lord Cornwallis, its large collection of 17th and 18th-century English furniture made a spectacular sale in 1982.

A view across fields near Danemore Park

To the west you can also see the mature oak and beech of Priest Wood (122) (TQ 537397), another of Kent's many important areas of ancient woodland, with mixed species also including hazel, birch, ash and hornbeam. In the nearby fields you can walk along green lanes (121) (TQ 540395), flanked by old hedgerows. Still providing links with the ancient woodland, the hedges have marked the field boundaries since Saxon times. Hedgerows have survived better in the High Weald than in the Low Weald, where fields have long covered a much wider acreage.

Langton Green

To the east, Scots pines mark Langton House (118) (TQ 542393) and Langton Green (119) (TQ 543393). Langton Green, like many others, gives the appearance of the traditional nuclear village, with houses and church encircling a large, immaculately kept green. Once this was the 'clearing in the forest', and in medieval times part of an important manor in the parish of Speldhurst, with Hollonds (TQ 542387), home of the 'Fair Maid of Kent' at its centre. It retained its old name of Lankington Green, based on the Saxon word for clearing, until 1864.

The surrounding land was much quarried for sandstone and gravel. One old sandstone quarry (TQ 544394) lies immediately north of the green. It is now an important wildlife site were many invertebrates have found a home among the fallen trees, and where many birds find a good food supply.

The village grew, however, around the farm, also to the north. The east side of the green became the centre, with cottages attached to the farm, the forge and the wheelwright's house.

The Church of All Saints (117) (TQ 542392) was built in 1862, in the Gothic Revival style, by Sir George Gilbert Scott, designer of the Albert Memorial and St Pancras Station and hotel. It contains, like St Mary's Speldhurst, fine stained glass windows by the pre-Raphaelites. William Morris designed the east window around 1862. Edward Burne-Jones designed the window showing St Alba and St Stephen in 1865. He designed the west window, showing St Mark, soon after.

The most imposing window was designed by Charles Kempe in 1904. This shows the Tree of Jesse, in unusually rich colours, spreading across five lancets. The vine-stem with its large leaves and tempting bunches of grapes, show well the exuberance of the late Victorian style. You will also see the reredos made of alabaster and, in the south chapel, a trowel and mallet made in Tunbridge Ware. Tunbridge Ware is the term used to describe furniture and other wooden artifacts decorated with mosaic inlay, using a mixture of local wood, such as beech, sycamore, yew, cherry, or plum. The work is intricate and highly polished and may have been known as early as the late 16th century.

Parklands

When you return to the High Weald Walk, you pass several houses built in the 19th century as the population expanded here. Ashurst Place (123) (TQ 540397), in 23 acres of mature parkland, now a home for the elderly, was built in the 1860s and soon became known as the base for the Ashurst Lodge Company for breeding horses. Many of the parkland trees were planted at that time.

Shirley Hall (124) (TQ 541399), now divided into flats, was built in the early-19th century. Known as Sherlock Hall for some time, this is one of the oldest occupied sites in the area, one of the few sites mentioned in the Domesday Book. The Stable Court, with an archway for entrance, was built around 1850.

At Danemore Park (126) (TQ 543406) you cross an avenue which runs for a third of a mile, lined with 100-year old chestnuts, oaks and limes. This links the main house, built in the 1830s in Georgian style, with Danemore Lodge (1860), built from sandstone in Tudor style. The area has many important habitats for wildlife.

The pasture is of an unusually high quality, not with the uniform, strong green achieved with fertiliser, but with the mottled effect which results from seasonal flowering and decline. In the summer you can see purple self heal and yellow rattle. This is a home too for the common spotted orchid.

Burnt Wood

As you go through Burnt Wood (127) (TQ 546406), you descend into the eastern portion of Avery's Wood (128) (TQ 541407), running along the slopes of a Wealden ghyll, part of an ancient woodland where little has altered over the centuries.

On the drier ground of Burnt Wood grow beech, sessile oak, holly and birch. Bluebells make a wonderful sight in the spring. Wood sorrel grows here and various ferns. On the damper slopes you will find ragged robin and purple self heal.

Lower down, at the base of the sandstone there are moist patches where the springs emerge and form flushes. Here you will find alder coppice and ash. On the drier patches, in between the flushes, grow pedunculate oak, hazel, ash and hornbeam, coppiced in places. The ground flora includes pendulous sedge, golden saxifrage and common woodland orchids. It is an area with a wealth of mosses and lichens.

INTERESTING FEATURES

113 Beech Wood

Beech Wood is a stretch of ancient woodland growing on the staggered fault lines of weathered sandstone. Sweet chestnut grows alongside yew and holly.

114 Top Hill Farm

Top Hill Farm has been a mixed farm for several centuries. It produces good cereal crops on relatively sandy soils.

115 A264

This road was once a busy packhorse lane linking Ashurst with Gipp's Cross. It was still known as Sandy Lane early this century.

Burnt Wood, off Bullingstone Lane

116 Langton Park Lodge

Park Lodge was once the lodge at the start of a long drive to Ashurst Park.

117 Church of All Saints

This Gothic Revival church was built in 1862 by Sir George Gilbert Scott. It contains stained glass windows by Sir Edward Burne-Jones, William Morris and Charles Kempe.

118 Langton House

This house was built in 1810 in the Regency style, as the new dower house for the manor.

119 Langton Green

The east side of the green became the centre of the village. Old buildings include:

Old wheelwright's cottage

A 16th-century building.

Old Birchett's

Timber-framed and underbuilt with brick, this house dates from the 17th century.

Common Spotted Orchid
Clover
Yellow Rattle
Bugle
Buttercups

The Forge,
Hollands Farmhouse and stable
These were all built in the early-19th century, of sandstone ashlar.

The 'Hare'
Once known as the 'Greyhound', the 'Hare' stands on the corner of the A264 and the Green.

120 Ashurst Park
Now a residential home known as Fernchase Manor, the house was built in the 1830s. Stone dressing covers red brick.

121 Green Lanes
The High Weald Walk passes between old hedgerows. These contain trees of ancient woodland, including hawthorn and hazel, and provide important habitats.

122 Priest Wood
Priest Wood forms another of Kent's important areas of ancient woodland. Bluebells grow in the old coppice area.

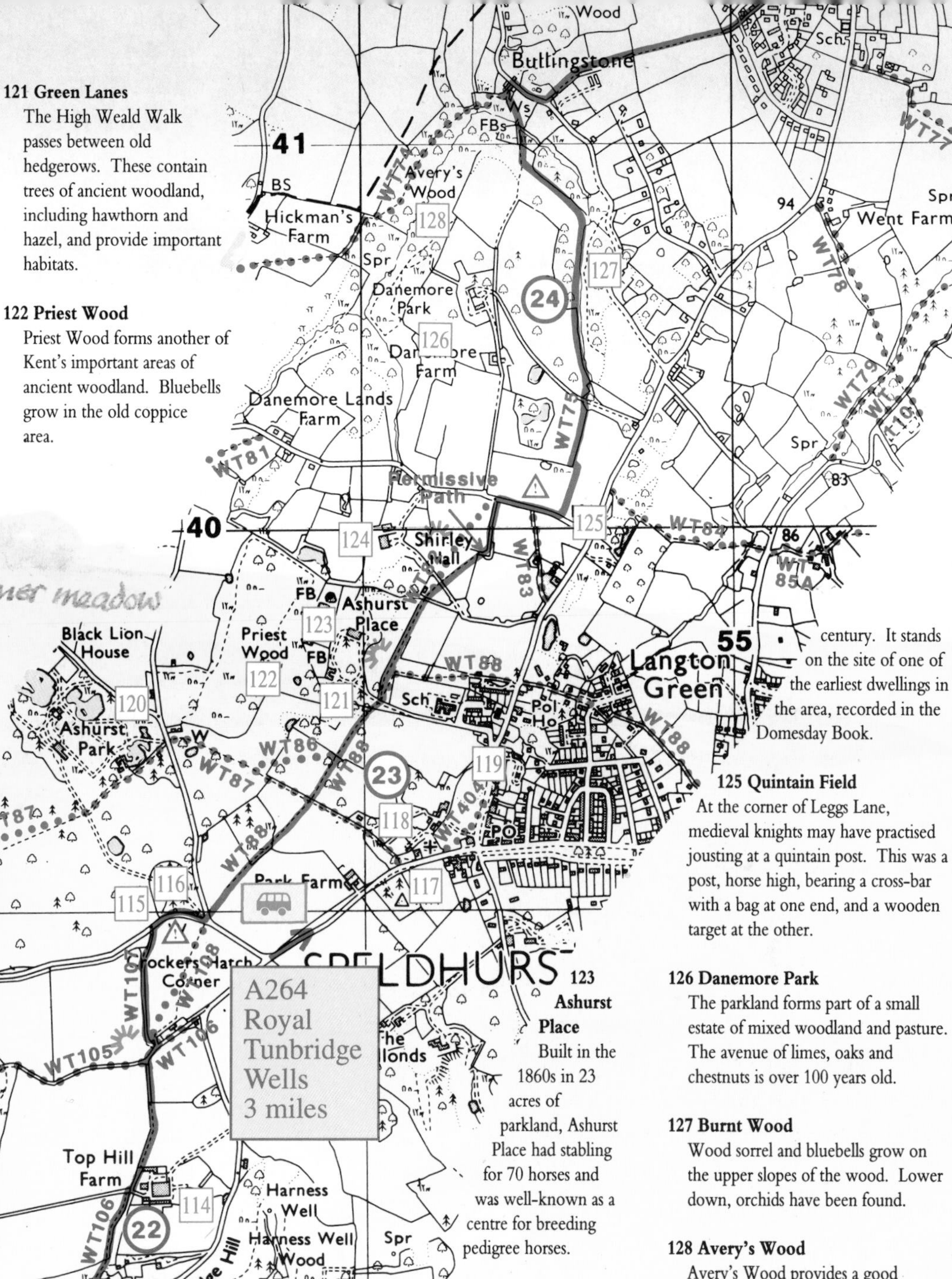

Danemore Park – summer meadow

123 Ashurst Place
Built in the 1860s in 23 acres of parkland, Ashurst Place had stabling for 70 horses and was well-known as a centre for breeding pedigree horses.

124 Shirley Hall
Now converted into flats, the house was built in the early-19th century. It stands on the site of one of the earliest dwellings in the area, recorded in the Domesday Book.

125 Quintain Field
At the corner of Leggs Lane, medieval knights may have practised jousting at a quintain post. This was a post, horse high, bearing a cross-bar with a bag at one end, and a wooden target at the other.

126 Danemore Park
The parkland forms part of a small estate of mixed woodland and pasture. The avenue of limes, oaks and chestnuts is over 100 years old.

127 Burnt Wood
Wood sorrel and bluebells grow on the upper slopes of the wood. Lower down, orchids have been found.

128 Avery's Wood
Avery's Wood provides a good example of ghyll woodland. Golden saxifrage, marsh valerian and the wood horsetail, equisetum sylvaticum, grow here.

8 LINK ROUTE 1

HIGH BROOMS *(railway station)* **- VIADUCT** *(Old Forge Farm)*

$1^1/_4$ miles - allow $^3/_4$ hour

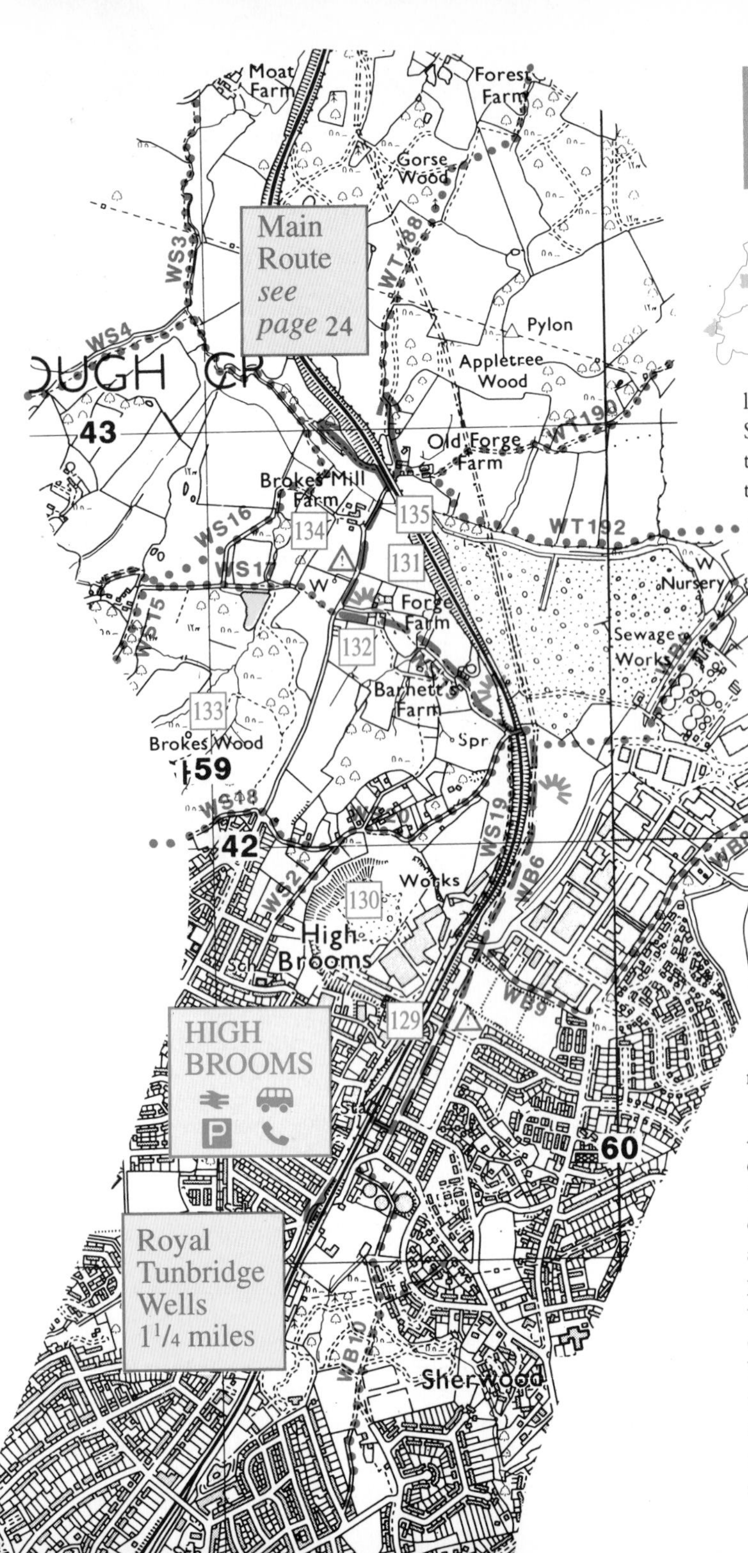

High Brooms

High Brooms (TQ 592416) lies between Powder Mill Lane and the railway line, to the south-east of Southborough. It takes its name from the broom bushes which once covered the slopes. At one time, gypsies who encamped here made brushes from the slender twigs. Though still heavily wooded in 1882, High Brooms has long been an industrial area.

The quarry (130) (TQ 594418) provided the stone for Penshurst Place, giving the old name, Quarrylands, to this part of the High Weald.

Industry

The Wadhurst Clay on the lower slopes combined with the woodland for fuel and the water for power to make this an important iron working area.

The Old Forge (134) (TQ 593428) worked with Vauxhall Furnace (TQ 592440) throughout most of the 17th century.

As the iron industry declined, forge owners sought other occupations. In 1772 the forge became a powder mill, one of only four in the country allowed to make a specially fine powder used by George III to shoot wildfowl. Within a few months, the original forge blew up. A new and better mill operated until 1845 when that too became redundant. Then a corn mill was established. This lasted until 1923. Trees now grow on the site of the mill ponds.

Also on the lower slopes small, hand-worked pits gradually emerged as people made bricks from the Wadhurst Clay. The High Brooms Brick and Tile Quarry was formed in 1885 and closed in 1968. Bricks were produced in many colours, with unique crests and medallions embossed on them. You can see some of these on older houses in the area.

The tall chimney at Forge Farm survives from an old brick kiln

Extensive house-building began in the 19th century as a result of expansion from Tunbridge Wells, and with the growth of the brick industry.

The copyholders of South Frith had protested loudly in the 16th century at the loss of their woodland to the iron industry. Brokes Wood (132) (TQ 590423) is the only large stretch of woodland which escaped the woodcutter's axe. Here you pass near a large area of ancient woodland, whose boundaries have changed little even since it was first marked out on the first Ordnance Survey map in 1801. It contains a wealth of wildlife, with birds, rare moths and butterflies.

INTERESTING FEATURES

129 The South Eastern Railway (SER)
The railway company was formed in 1835 to build a line from London to Dover, and brought a branch line from Tonbridge as far as High Brooms in 1845. This tunnelled on to Tunbridge Wells in 1846, and reached Hastings in 1851.

130 Quarry
This quarry was said to be the biggest in the country. In it were found fossils 120 million years old which helped to date the geology of the region. Now it is a fishing pond, with good wildlife.

131 Tall chimney
In the grounds of Forge Farm a tall chimney survives from an old brick kiln. An arched tunnel within the kiln now serves as a cow shed.

132 Powder Mill Lane
The lane takes its name from the gunpowder mill which took over the old forge when that became redundant. The first mill blew up soon after, a second survived until 1845.

133 Brokes Wood
The boundaries of the wood have remained intact at least since the first Ordnance Survey map appeared in 1801. It is an important conservation area for wildlife.

134 Brokes Mill Farm
The farm stands beside the site of the old forge. The forge was first built in 1553 by David Willard on land owned by Sir Thomas Fane. Between 1623 and 1679 the forge worked in conjunction with Vauxhall Furnace lower down the valley.

135 Viaduct
When the viaduct was built in 1845, construction scattered most traces of forge cinder from the valley.

The viaduct at Old Forge Farm was built in 1845

9 LINK ROUTE 2

Mount Sion *(Royal Tunbridge Wells)* - High Wood

1½ miles - allow ¾ hour

Royal Tunbridge Wells

Royal Tunbridge Wells owes its presence to one feature alone, its chalybeate spring. Until the early-17th century this corner of the High Weald consisted of rough pasture, interspersed with iron workings and small villages. In 1606 Lord North was returning from a stay at Eridge Park. In a valley where three parishes, Frant, Speldhurst and Tonbridge, all met, he saw a small spring with the brownish tinge to it he recognised from spa water elsewhere. A year later he returned, drank again and felt better for it. From time to time visitors came to taste the waters. Henrietta Maria, wife of Charles I arrived in 1630, staying with her entourage in tents on the common. Charles II brought his court in 1663. Nell Gwyn came too, probably giving rise to the title 'Les eaux de scandale'.

Only in 1680 did proper building begin, first on the north side of the common, and next around the site of the spring, the place known as The Pantiles (TQ 581387). In 1684, Lady Musquerry of Somerhill who owned the manor of South Frith, leased out her land for building, and development began on the slopes of Mount Sion (TQ 584388).

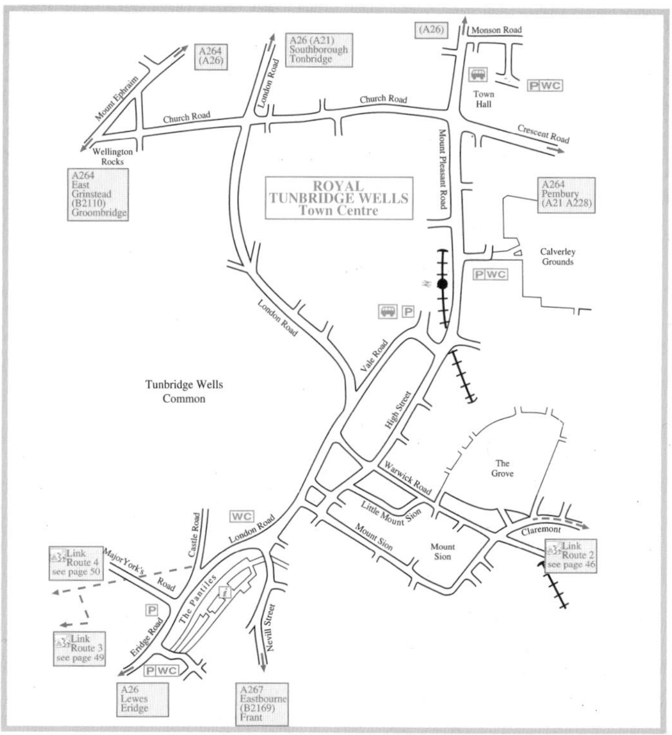

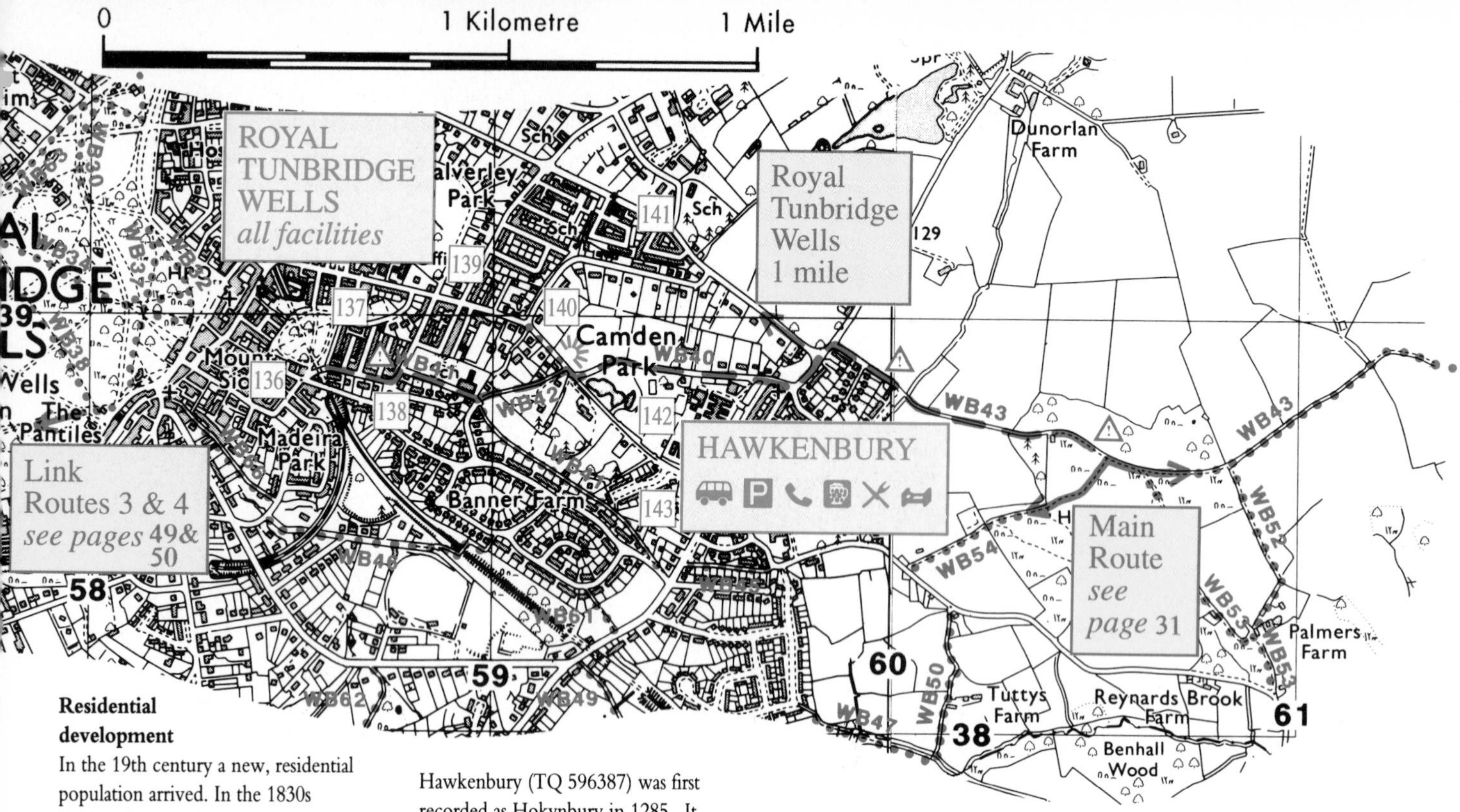

Residential development

In the 19th century a new, residential population arrived. In the 1830s Decimus Burton designed the Calverley estate (139) (TQ 588392) on the eastern slopes. His builder, William Willicombe, may have been responsible for Camden Park (140) (TQ 594390), as well as Lansdowne Road and Mount Ephraim Road. At the northern end of the open space of Camden Park you will find wild flowers such as buttercup, stitchwort and wood sorrel. In the south-western corner, where there is a small bog, you will find soft rush, bugle and cuckoo flower. Among the ornamental hedges are hawthorn, Scots pine and silver birch. A wide range of birds inhabit the Park. In Claremont Road you can see the rear elevations of houses built in the 1830s, whose bow-fronts look on to Grove Hill Road. Together with Nevill Park (TQ 570391) and Hungershall Park (TQ 572387), all form part of an important conservation area.

Hawkenbury (TQ 596387) was first recorded as Hokynbury in 1285. It was generally known as Tutty's Village during the 18th and 19th centuries.

INTERESTING FEATURES

136 Mount Sion

Like Mount Ephraim, the slope was given its name by the Puritans. It was the first area of importance to be built and became the centre from the end of the 17th century. Jerningham House is the oldest house, unusual with its total cover of hung tiles.

137 The Grove

The open space was designed in 1707 by the Duke of Buckingham. The lime and beech trees have taken over where oaks originally stood.

138 Houses in Claremont Road

The houses were laid out in a curve in the 1830s. Their frontages face on to Grove Hill Road.

139 Calverley Park

Built by Decimus Burton in 1828 as an early 'garden suburb', it has a unified scheme of villas and terraces, built mainly in Classical style, overlooking the bowl of the hill from Mount Pleasant.

Little Mount Sion, near the start of the link route to Hawkenbury

140 Camden Park

The houses of Camden Park, in white brick or stone, follow the style of Decimus Burton.

141 St Peter's Church

The church can be seen from just south of Pembury bypass. It was built from local sandstone in 1874-6 in the Victorian Decorated style, as Tunbridge Wells spread outwards and in response to the needs of Tutty's Village.

142 Land Registry Offices

These offices, built in 1963, form a conspicuous landmark which can be seen from many of the surrounding slopes.

143 'Spread Eagle'

One of the few surviving buildings from the last century, the 'Spread Eagle' has an old mounting block in the forecourt.

10 LINK ROUTE 3

Tunbridge Wells Common - Groombridge Place

$3^1/_2$ miles - allow $1^3/_4$ hours

Below the common, in the south-west, the River Grom emerges from a culvert to take a meandering course down the valley and join the River Medway east of Burrswood at TQ 512376.

The countryside stretches almost to the centre of Tunbridge Wells

Friezland Wood

Friezland Wood (150) (TQ 565383) covering nearly 20 acres, is semi-natural ancient woodland, with a wide range of mosses and lichens on the rocks surviving in the same, humid 'Atlantic' micro-climate that you find at Eridge Rocks. You will find a mixture of broadleaved trees including oak, ash, holly and yew, alder, hazel and willow. The wood supports golden saxifrage and wood sedge. In less damp areas you will also find wood sorrel.

High Rocks

In a narrow defile lie High Rocks (152) (TQ 558383), the tallest outcrop of Ardingly sandstone in the region, and a well-known tourist attraction for over 300 years. With bare, rounded tops and vertical sides, they present a remarkable sight. You will see that the concave or convex sides of the rocks match one another, presumably having been split apart by earth movements.

The darker patches result from the hardening of the surface around organic matter from surface vegetation and from iron oxides and silica. The distinctive honeycomb weathering is generally believed to be the result of salt emerging from inside before evaporating.

Mesolithic people sheltered in a series of rock shelters (TQ 561383) at the base, leaving hand-axes, dating from around 4500 BC. Above lie the damaged remains of a 20-acre promontory fort (153) (TQ 561382), built by Iron Age Celts in a form similar to the fort at Castle Hill and used for defence.

Adam's Well

At Adam's Well (158) (TQ 549383), it is worth walking up Barrow Lane (157) (TQ 567386) to see the heavily weathered sandstone strata of this narrow ghyll. Here you can see how successive layers of silts accumulated in the ancient delta before the earth movements that created this landscape. The track used to be the packhorse lane, running northwards from Adam's Well, via Gipps Cross (TQ 550392), once Gibbets Cross. The many springs along the way provided welcome refreshment.

Adam's Well was famous long before the spring at Tunbridge Wells was discovered, its water considered especially fresh and pure. Medieval brick surrounds were unearthed in the 18th century.

In the area around Hollonds Wood (TQ 542384), in the 13th century, lived Joanna, the 'Fair Maid of Kent'. The daughter of the Earl of Kent and grand-daughter of Edward I, she was briefly married to Sir Thomas Hollond, Lord of the Manor of Speldhurst.

After his death she married Edward, the Black Prince, her cousin and love of her earlier years. It was her misadventure with a stocking-garter that led to the foundation of the Order of that name.

A small footbridge (TQ 539378) below Harness Well Wood marks the edge of the Groombridge Place estate.

INTERESTING FEATURES

144 Tunbridge Wells West Station
This station was built in 1866 in polychrome brick, with clock tower and platform canopy, when the line from East Grinstead was extended through Groombridge by the London Brighton and the South Coast Railway. It is now a restaurant. The Tunbridge Wells and Eridge Railway Preservation Society (TWERPS) plan to restore the line and establish a steam railway.

145 Brook
Emerging from a culvert to become the River Grom, the small stream used to mark the county boundary here in Royal Tunbridge Wells, as it still does further west.

146 Broadwater Down
This area was first developed in the 1860s. Forty-four houses were built, many now converted into flats or demolished for newer residences.

147 St Mark's Church
The spire of St Mark's Church, built in sandstone between 1864-66, provides a landmark for miles around. The church combines Victorian Decorated style with the architect's own ideas.

148 Hungershall Park
The area was developed with the building of good quality residences on land originally belonging to the Abergavenny estates, during the mid-Victorian period of expansion. The houses look north across a valley to Nevill Park (TQ 570391).

The Pantiles, the historic heart of Royal Tunbridge Wells

The High Rocks Inn. The tall sandstone outcrop opposite has been a tourist attraction for 300 years

149 Ramslye

First mentioned in 1262 as Remese, there was an early settlement on these slopes. Herdsmen came here from further afield to enjoy the rights of pannage.

150 Friezland Wood

The wood is an area of semi-natural ancient woodland where the moist atmosphere from water-retentive sandstone under a woodland canopy has preserved an 'Atlantic' micro-climate similar to that at Eridge Rocks. Friezland Wood was purchased in 1986 by the Woodland Trust with grant aid from Tunbridge Wells Borough Council. BTCV volunteers help the Trust with the management of the wood.

Pipistrelle Bat

151 High Rocks Halt

The halt opened as a railway stop in June 1907, and closed in May 1952. The down platform was on the east side of the road bridge.

152 High Rocks

These rocks present the tallest sandstone outcrops of the region. Middle Stone Age people used the hollows under the rocks as shelter, around 4,500 BC.

153 High Rocks Fort

The hilltop provided a stronghold for Iron Age Celts from around 100BC. Their successors added fortifications to defend themselves against the Romans during the Claudian invasions of AD 45.

154 High Rocks Inn

The inn became a popular resting place from where to visit pleasure gardens laid out in the last century. Bridges, bowling greens and a maze were among the attractions added to this ancient site.

155 Broadwater Forest

A former heathland site with numerous ghylls and springs, the forest used to be part of the Waterdown Forest. Replanted this century, mainly with conifers, it still contains a variety of important habitats.

156 Holmewood

This country house was built by Decimus Burton in classical style, first in 1827, then again, after a fire, in 1837, on the site of a Tudor farmhouse.

157 Barrow Lane

In medieval times a packhorse lane ran past several springs including Adam's Well. It was part of a long-distance route between the south coast and London.

158 Adam's Well

The chalybeate spring, which emerged here, was known for its water's remarkable purity long before Tunbridge Wells developed.

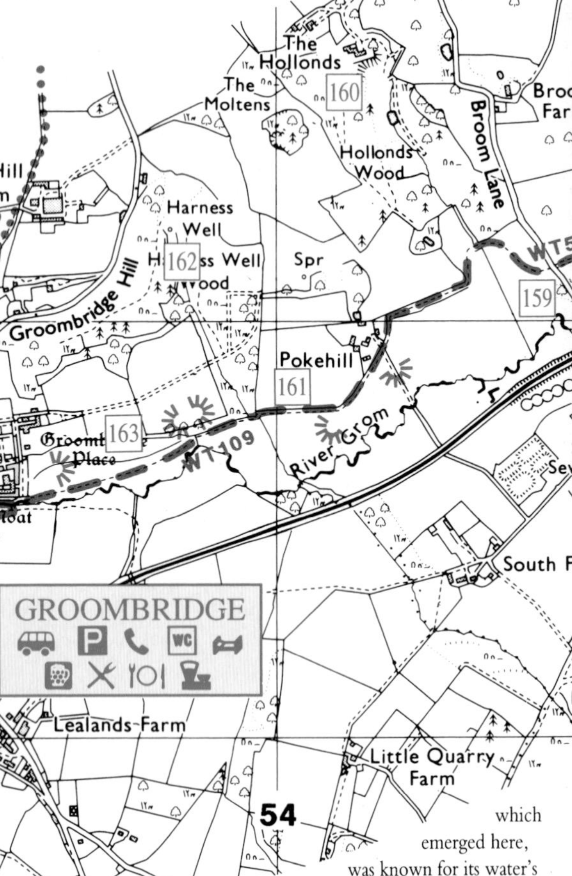

159 Broom Lane

This lane served as the route used in medieval times by the knights of Groombridge Place on their way to church at Speldhurst.

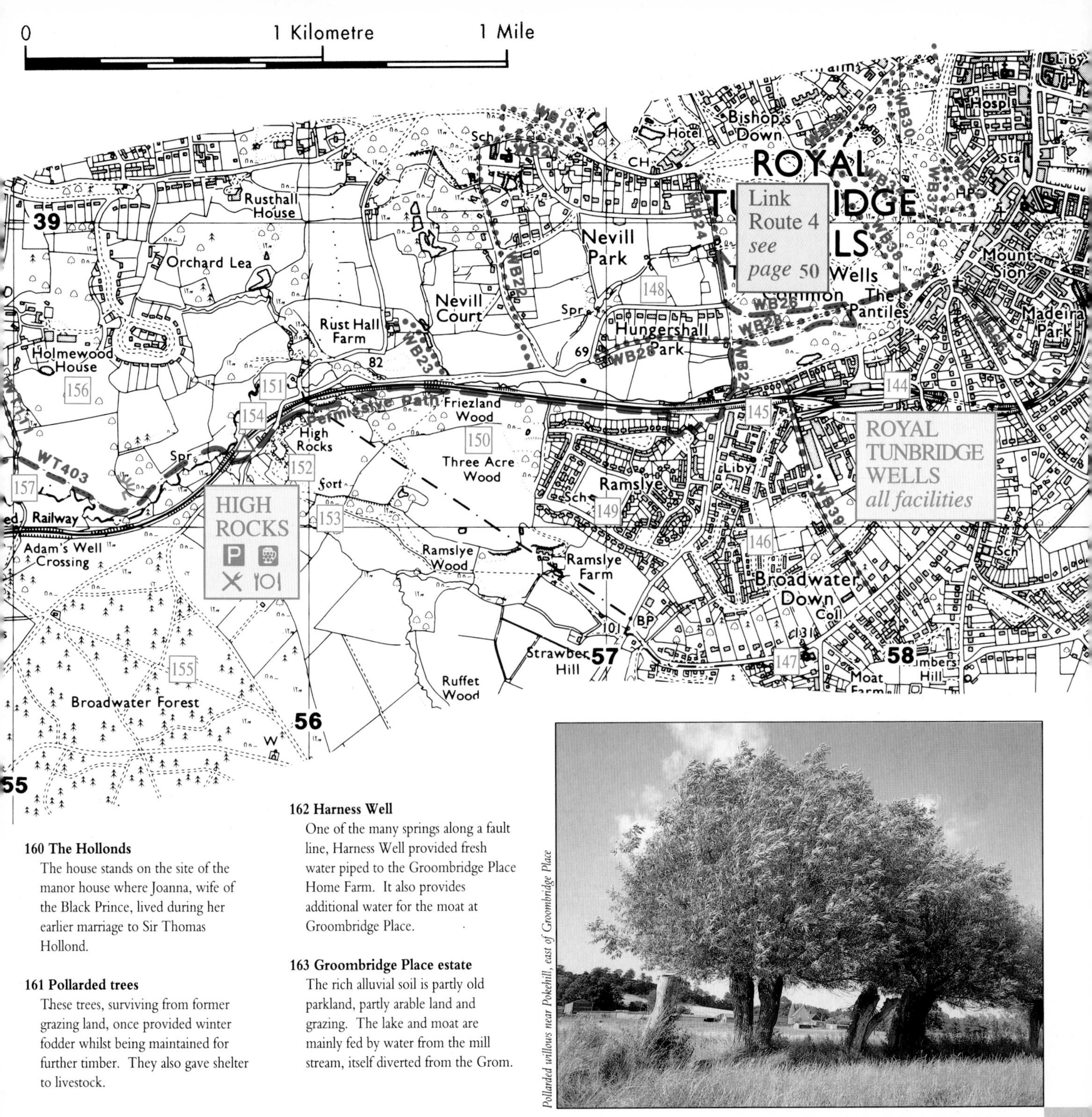

160 The Hollonds
The house stands on the site of the manor house where Joanna, wife of the Black Prince, lived during her earlier marriage to Sir Thomas Hollond.

161 Pollarded trees
These trees, surviving from former grazing land, once provided winter fodder whilst being maintained for further timber. They also gave shelter to livestock.

162 Harness Well
One of the many springs along a fault line, Harness Well provided fresh water piped to the Groombridge Place Home Farm. It also provides additional water for the moat at Groombridge Place.

163 Groombridge Place estate
The rich alluvial soil is partly old parkland, partly arable land and grazing. The lake and moat are mainly fed by water from the mill stream, itself diverted from the Grom.

Pollarded willows near Pokehill, east of Groombridge Place

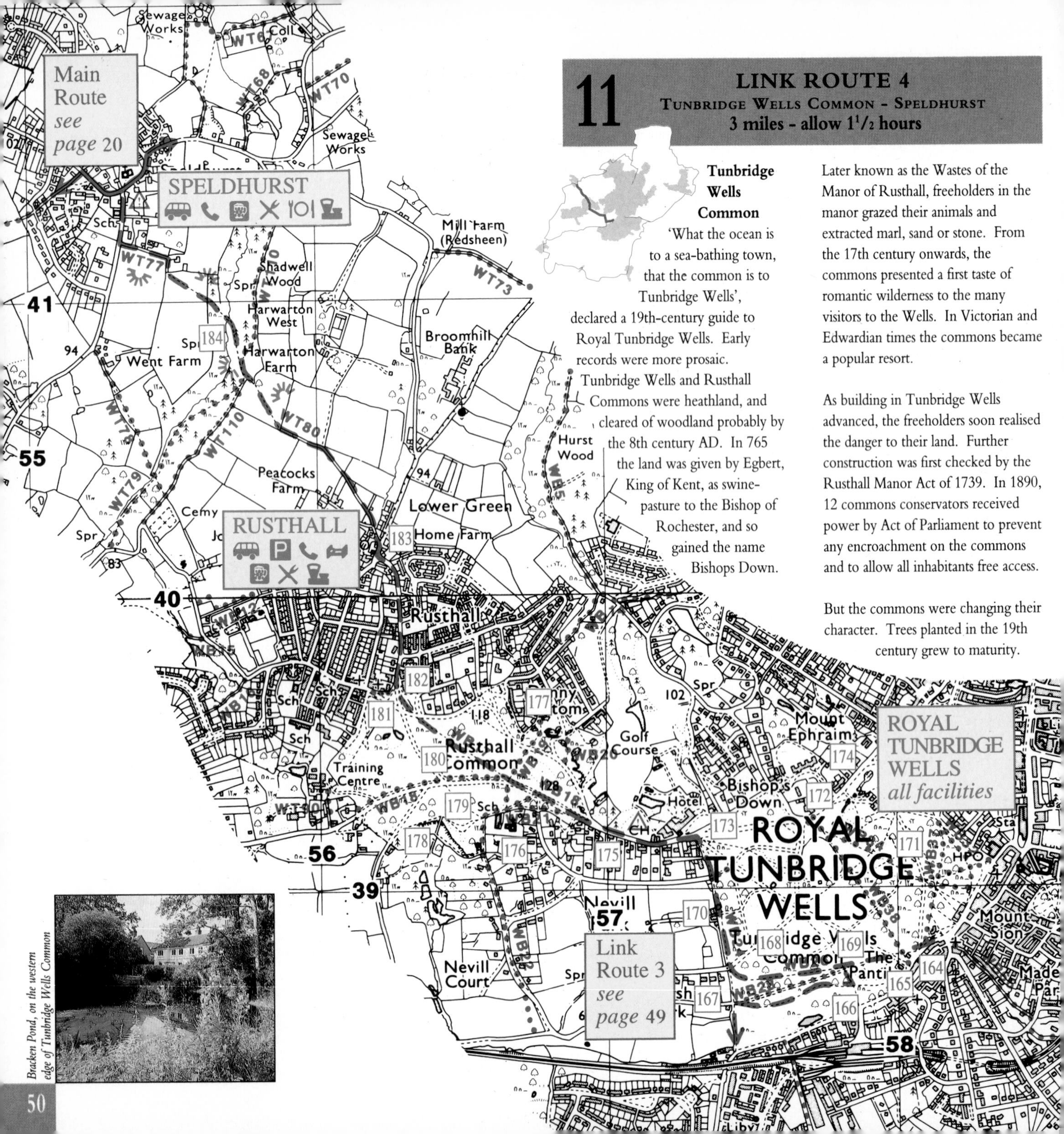

11

LINK ROUTE 4

Tunbridge Wells Common - Speldhurst

3 miles - allow $1^1/_2$ hours

Tunbridge Wells Common

'What the ocean is to a sea-bathing town, that the common is to Tunbridge Wells', declared a 19th-century guide to Royal Tunbridge Wells. Early records were more prosaic. Tunbridge Wells and Rusthall Commons were heathland, and cleared of woodland probably by the 8th century AD. In 765 the land was given by Egbert, King of Kent, as swine-pasture to the Bishop of Rochester, and so gained the name Bishops Down.

Later known as the Wastes of the Manor of Rusthall, freeholders in the manor grazed their animals and extracted marl, sand or stone. From the 17th century onwards, the commons presented a first taste of romantic wilderness to the many visitors to the Wells. In Victorian and Edwardian times the commons became a popular resort.

As building in Tunbridge Wells advanced, the freeholders soon realised the danger to their land. Further construction was first checked by the Rusthall Manor Act of 1739. In 1890, 12 commons conservators received power by Act of Parliament to prevent any encroachment on the commons and to allow all inhabitants free access.

But the commons were changing their character. Trees planted in the 19th century grew to maturity.

Bracken Pond, on the western edge of Tunbridge Wells Common

Toad Rock, an unusually-shaped weathered block of Ardingly sandstone

Grazing, in decline since 1918, finally ended during the Second World War. A new tree cover had developed, ponds had silted up, scrub began to spread. Only in recent years, particularly after the 1987 storm, did it become apparent how much of the old heathland habitat had been lost.

Now, following a plan proposed by the Kent Trust for Nature Conservation, and adopted in 1992, the conservators are working to restore the mixture of plant and animal life unique to the acid heathland. They aim to keep the historic relationship between town and commons.

Rusthall

The name of Rusthall or Rustwell, from the brown colour of the water rust arising from its iron content, first appeared in the eighth century. The best known of the Lords of this manor was Elias de Rust who lived at the beginning of the 13th century. His house may have stood to the north of Bishops Down.

It was here, during the Civil Wars, that the Roundheads gained a firm footing. Cromwell settled many of his men on Mount Ephraim and on Mounts Calverley and Sion, just over the Tonbridge border, when the Royalists placed themselves in Southborough.

The old packhorse lane which passes Adam's Well further south continues along here on its way north. The High Weald Walk crosses it at TQ 577407. In Shadwell Wood lay Chad's Well, one of the many springs that made the route attractive to travellers.

INTERESTING FEATURES

164 Milestone

The stone dates from the early-19th century. Now illegible, it marked 36 miles to London.

165 York Cottage

This cottage, with full weatherboarding, dates from the mid-19th century. It is one of the few houses to be built on the common.

166 Brighton Lake

The lake is fed by a chalybeate spring and was enlarged in 1858 by workers given employment by the minister of King Charles' church, William Law Pope. It soon became known as Pope's Puddle.

167 Cottage

The present cottage stands on the site of a late-17th century or early-18th century cottage known as Kentish Cottage. The well-known Scottish preacher and minister, Dr John Cumming, used it as a summer home from where he wrote regularly to 'The Times'.

168 Disused Race Course

Appearing first on a map of 1738, the race course was last used in the early 1860s.

169 Terrace Walk

The walk was created by the workers who enlarged Brighton Lake. It became a 'Greensward terrace walk' above the pond.

170 Bracken Cottage Pond

The pond has been reinstated as part of the on-going work to restore the commons. It is one of several ponds formerly kept as watering places for sheep and cattle.

171 Royal Victoria Grove

Consisting of a double line of limes, sycamores and elms the Grove was planted in 1835 to commemorate visits by Princess Victoria and her mother, the Duchess of Kent. A third row was added in 1992, the 40th anniversary of the reign of Queen Elizabeth II.

The 'Red Lion' at Lower Green, said to be the oldest licensed pub in Kent

172 Wellington Rocks
These rocks were named after the hotel which stood to the north. This was named in 1875, when first opened, after the Duke of Wellington whom the first owner, John Braby, had admired.

173 Bishop's Down
Still keeping the ancient name of the common, Bishops Down recalls King Egbert's gift to the Bishop of Rochester.

174 Mount Ephraim
First named by the Puritans in the 17th century, the road runs along a turf walk originally levelled in 1881.

175 Nevill Park
The development was started in the 1840s on Abergavenny land. Its houses look southwards over the small valley towards the other Abergavenny development, Hungershall Park.

176 St Paul's Church
Built in local sandstone in 1849-50, it incorporates a number of Victorian Gothic styles, such as sharply pointed Early English arches to the arcades, but with heavy foliage on the capitals. The Decorated west window was added in 1918.

St Paul's churchyard is now an important conservation area for wildlife. The growth of grass, trimmed only in autumn, allows wood anemones, wood sorrel, lady's smock and primroses to flourish.

177 Toad Rock
An isolated block of Ardingly Sandstone, the rock was formed like Eridge Rocks and High Rocks, by the weathering of softer deposits. Nearby stand others, given names by the Victorians, such as the Lion and the Loaf around it.

The Toad Rock Retreat and the Toad Rock Tavern
These are the last surviving of several pubs bearing the name of the Rock. Also selling beer in the 1880s was the Toad Rock Cottage.

Denny Bottom
Denny Bottom was one of the places where freeholders in the Manor of Rusthall could quarry and dig for marl.

178 Happy Valley
This area was the site of pleasure grounds in the early-18th century. It became a well-known beauty spot in Victorian times.

179 Rusthall Common
The northern common is mainly covered by secondary woodland and scrub. Hawthorn, young oak, sycamore and birch are well established, but pockets of bell heather still exist, along with colonies of flowers such as bluebells and wood anemones.

180 The cricket ground
First levelled to a reasonable standard in the late-19th century, the cricket ground had seen cricket played here well before that.

The Assembly Room
The Assembly Room, built in 1655 for the first visitors to the Wells, stood on the site of an old pit.

181 Two Yews Cottage
Built in 1571, the cottage is the oldest house in Rusthall.

182 Old Coach Road
This important road ran northwards along the line of the Lower Green Road.

183 Lower Green, Rusthall
A community has existed around the Lower Green since the Middle Ages.

'Red Lion'
First licensed around 1415, this public house is said to be said to be the oldest licensed public house in Kent. New brick buildings replaced its thatched coach house and stables in 1895.

184 Sproud's Wood
The long, narrow ghyll of Sproud's Wood was severely storm damaged in 1987. New trees are now becoming established.

The link route to Speldhurst passes through Sproud's Wood

still be found in the High Weald

Interesting Places to Visit

On or near the High Weald Walk

Badsell Park Farm Trail
Matfield
☎ Paddock Wood (0892) 832549

Bartley Mill
Near Frant
☎ Lamberhurst (0892) 890372

Bayham Abbey
Near Lamberhurst
☎ Lamberhurst (0892) 890381

David Salomons House
Etherington Hill
Southborough
☎ Tunbridge Wells (0892) 515152

Day at the Wells (A)
The Corn Exchange
The Pantiles
Royal Tunbridge Wells
☎ Tunbridge Wells (0892) 546545

Groombridge Place Gardens
Groombridge
☎ Tunbridge Wells (0892) 863999

Pantiles (The) and Bath Square
Royal Tunbridge Wells

Spa Valley Railway
(Tunbridge Wells & Eridge Railway Preservation Society)
Eridge Station
Eridge Green
Royal Tunbridge Wells
☎ Tunbridge Wells (0892) 862140

Tonbridge Castle
Tonbridge
☎ Tonbridge (0732) 770929

Tunbridge Wells Museum and Art Gallery
Mount Pleasant Road
Royal Tunbridge Wells
☎ Tunbridge Wells (0892) 526121

Parish Churches
(Keys usually obtained locally if not open)

Countryside Open Spaces

On or near the High Weald Walk

Birchden and Aytton's Woods
Groombridge
☎ Cranbrook (0580) 211044

Friezland Wood
High Rocks Lane
Royal Tunbridge Wells
☎ Grantham (0476) 74297

Harrison's Rocks
Groombridge
☎ Tunbridge Wells (0892) 864238
Please note that the sandstone outcrop is privately owned by the British Mountaineering Council. Climbing is a dangerous sport; visitors and walkers should avoid going near the climbers or their equipment.

High Rocks
High Rocks Lane
Royal Tunbridge Wells
☎ Tunbridge Wells (0892) 526074

Hurst Wood
Royal Tunbridge Wells
☎ Grantham (0476) 74297

Rusthall Common and Toad Rock
Royal Tunbridge Wells
☎ Tunbridge Wells (0982) 526121

Southborough Common
Southborough
☎ Tunbridge Wells (0892) 529176

Tudeley Woods
Tudeley
☎ Shoreham-by-Sea (0273) 463642

Tunbridge Wells Common and Wellington Rocks
Royal Tunbridge Wells
☎ Tunbridge Wells (0892) 526121

Other Walking Opportunities

If you have enjoyed this walk and would like to explore other waymarked walking routes in Kent, write to the Access and Recreation Officer (listed elsewhere) for an information pack. For details of recreational paths in East Sussex write to the Access Project (listed elsewhere).

In series with the 'High Weald Walk' are the 'Stour Valley Walk', 'Eden Valley Walk', 'Greensand Way' and 'Elham Valley Way'. Other route guidebooks are planned and in preparation.

Copies of these or any other walking guides can be obtained from bookshops, libraries, tourist information centres and the Access and Recreation Officer.

It is possible for you to devise your own shorter linear and circular walks using the extensive rights of way network throughout the counties. Information about these can be obtained by studying either the Ordnance Survey Pathfinder maps or the County Council Definitive Maps of Public Rights of Way. Copies of the latter can be inspected at public libraries or district council offices. In the event of difficulty please contact the Public Rights of Way Manager (listed elsewhere) in Kent or the Public Rights of Way Officer, Highways and Transportation Department, East Sussex County Council, Sackville House, Brooks Close, Lewes, East Sussex, ☎ Lewes (0273) 482250.

Linked, or running close, to the High Weald Walk are a number of other walks, as follows:

Wealdway

Wealdway is an 80-mile linear route from the Thames Estuary at Gravesend to the English Channel at Beachy Head (Eastbourne). It crosses the North and South Downs and Kent and Sussex Weald. Between Stockland Green and Bullingstone it coincides with the High Weald Walk.

Publications:
'Wealdway' - Geoffrey King, Wealdway Group, c/o 11 Old London Road, Brighton, East Sussex BN1 8XR
'Wealdway Accommodation Guide' - Wealdway Group, as above.
'Guide to the Wealdway' - John H Mason, Constable and Co, 11 Orange Street, London WC2H 3EW.
'The Wealdway and the Vanguard Way' - Kev Reynolds, Cicerone Press, 2 Police Square, Milnthorpe, Cumbria.

Eden Valley Walk

A 15-mile linear walk between Tonbridge and Edenbridge. Upstream the route follows the River Eden as it meanders through a flat pastoral landscape. Historic houses, set in undulating parkland are passed en route, whilst downstream the route keeps company with the River Medway through Haysden Country Park.

Publication:
'Eden Valley Walk' - Kent County Council, Planning Department, Springfield, Maidstone, Kent ME14 2LX.

Sussex Border Path

The Path which follows rights of way close to the Sussex border with Hampshire, Surrey and Kent runs for nearly 150 miles between Emsworth and Rye. The route crosses the Weald through areas of woodland, farmland and heathland. At its closest, the route is four miles south-west of the High Weald Walk at Groombridge.

Publication:
'The Sussex Border Path Map Pack' - Ben Perkins and Aeneas Mackintosh, Ben Perkins, 11 Old London Road, Brighton, East Sussex BN1 8XR.

Forest Way

The Way has been developed as a linear Country Park along the trackbed of a former branch railway between East Grinstead and Ashurst junction, Groombridge. It runs along the Medway Valley from where there are views of Ashdown Forest to the south. At its closest, the route is four miles west of the High Weald Walk at Groombridge.

Publication:
'The Forest Way Country Park & Circular Walks' leaflet - High Weald Conservation Project (listed elsewhere).

Further Reading and References

(Selected list)

Batsford Guide to the Industrial Archaeology of South East England, (The)
A J Haselfoot
Batsford

Buildings of England (The): Sussex
I Nairn and N Pevsner
Penguin

Buildings of England (The): West Kent and the Weald of Kent
J Newman and N Pevsner
Penguin

Frant: The Story of a Wealden Parish
Patricia Wright
Frant Publications Project

History of Pembury
Mary Standen (author & publisher)

History of the County of Kent (A)
Edward Hasted
EP Publishing Ltd, London

Iron Industry of the Weald (The)
H Cleere and D Crossley
Leicester University Press

Kent History Illustrated
F W Jessup
Kent County Council

Pembury in the Past
Mary Standen
Meresborough Books

Royal Tunbridge Wells
Roger Farthing
Phillimore and Co Ltd

Tunbridge Wells and Rusthall Commons Past and Present
Ian Beavis
Tunbridge Wells Museum and Art Gallery

Weald (The)
S W Wooldridge and F Goldring
Collins

Weald (The)
W Gibbons
Unwin

Weald of Kent and Sussex
Sheila Kaye-Smith
Robert Hale Ltd

The attractive village green at Frant

Countryside Access Charter

Your rights of way are:

- Public footpaths - on foot only.
- Bridleways - on foot, horseback and pedal cycle.
- Byways - (usually old roads), most 'roads used as public paths' and, of course public roads - all traffic.

Use maps, signs and waymarks. Ordnance Survey Pathfinder and Landranger maps show most public rights of way.

On rights of way you can:

- Take a pram, pushchair or wheelchair if practicable.
- Take a dog (on a lead or under close control).
- Take a short route round an illegal obstruction or remove it sufficiently to get past.

You have a right to go for recreaton to:

- Public parks and open spaces - on foot.

have a profusion of flowers in spring

- ❖ Most commons near older towns and cities - on foot and sometimes on horseback.
- ❖ Private land where the owner has a formal agreement with the local authority.

In addition you can use the following by local or established custom or consent - ask for advice if you are unsure:

- ❖ Many areas of open country like moorland, fell and coastal areas, especially those of the National Trust, and most commons.
- ❖ Some woods and forests, especially those owned by the Forestry Commission.
- ❖ Country parks and picnic sites.
- ❖ Most beaches.
- ❖ Towpaths on canals and rivers.
- ❖ Some land that is being rested from agriculture, where notices allowing access are displayed.
- ❖ Some private paths and tracks.

Consent sometimes extends to riding horses and pedal cycles.

For your information

- ❖ County and metropolitan district councils and London boroughs have a duty to protect, maintain and record rights of way, and hold registers of commons and village greens - report problems you find to them.
- ❖ Obstructions, dangerous animals, harassment and misleading signs on rights of way are illegal.
- ❖ If a public path runs along the edge of a field, it must not be ploughed or disturbed.
- ❖ A public path across a field can be ploughed or disturbed to cultivate a crop, but the surface must be quickly restored and the line of the path made apparent on the ground.
- ❖ Crops (other than grass) must not be allowed to inconvenience the use of a rights of way, or present the line from being apparent on the ground.
- ❖ Landowners can require you to leave land to which you have no right of access.
- ❖ Motor vehicles are normally permitted only on roads, byways and some 'roads used as public paths'.
- ❖ Follow any local bylaws.

And, wherever you go, follow the Country Code

- ❖ Enjoy the countryside and respect its life and work.
- ❖ Guard against all risk of fire.
- ❖ Fasten all gates.
- ❖ Keep your dogs under close control.
- ❖ Keep to public paths across farmland.
- ❖ Use gates and stiles to cross fences, hedges and walls.
- ❖ Leave livestock, crops and machinery alone.
- ❖ Take your litter home.
- ❖ Help to keep all water clean.
- ❖ Protect wildlife, plants and trees.
- ❖ Take special care on country roads.
- ❖ Make no unnecessary noise.

This Charter is for practical guidance in England and Wales only. Fuller advice is given in a free booklet 'Out in the Country' available from Countryside Commission Postal Sales, PO Box 124, Walgrave, Northampton NN6 9TL, telephone (0604) 781848. Published with kind permission of the Countryside Commission.

Table of Historical Periods

Mesolithic	10000 - 3500BC}	
Neolithic	3500 - 2000BC}	Prehistoric
Bronze Age	2000 - 800BC}	
Iron Age	800BC - AD43}	
Roman	43 - 410	
Anglo Saxon	410 - 1066	
Norman	1066 - 1154	
Plantagenets	1154 - 1399}	
Lancastrians	1399 - 1461}	Medieval
Yorkists	1461 - 1485}	
Tudors	1485 - 1603}	
Elizabethan	1558 - 1603	Renaissance
Stuarts	1603 - 1714}	
Jacobean	1603 - 1649	
Commonwealth	1649 - 1660	
Restoration	1660 - 1702	
Anne	1702 - 1714	
Hanoverian	1714 - 1901	
Georgian	1714 - 1837	
Regency	1810 - 1820	
Victorian	1837 - 1901	
Edwardian	1901 - 1910	
Windsor	1910 - Present Day	

Table of Architectural Periods

Romanesque	1066 - 1190	
Early English	1190 - 1280}	
Decorated	1280 - 1380}	Gothic
Perpendicular	1380 - 1550}	
Classical	1550 - 1810	
Gothic & Classical Revivals	1810 - 1914	
Modern	1914 - Present Day	

ACKNOWLEDGEMENTS

We are grateful to the following for their assistance in route development and in the preparation of this guidebook:

Town and Parish Councils
Kent Trust for Nature Conservation
Sussex Wildlife Trust
Royal Society for the Protection of Birds
Woodland Trust
British Trust for Conservation Volunteers
British Mountaineering Council (Harrison's Rocks)
Kent High Weald Project Midweek and Weekend Volunteers
East Sussex County Council Recreation and Countryside Management Service
(Rangers, Employment Training Team and Volunteers)
Operation Raleigh
Bethany, The Skinners' and Tonbridge Schools, and West Kent College
Local Rambling Groups
Tunbridge Wells Commons Conservators
Middleton Press

The development, interpretation and promotion of the High Weald Walk has been achieved with financial assistance from the Countryside Commission.